D1420712

DESIGNS FOR THE SMALLER GARDEN

DESIGNS FOR THE SMALLER GARDEN

by **Donald Farthing** and
Guy Farthing R.I.B.A.,
Diploma in Landscape Architecture

W. Foulsham & Co. Ltd.
London · New York · Toronto · Cape Town · Sydney.

W FOULSHAM & COMPANY LIMITED
Yeovil Road, SLOUGH, Berkshire SL1 4JH

ISBN 0-572-01049-4

Printed in Hong Kong

Contents

Introduction

Ask a young couple what kind of garden they would most like to own and the chances are you will get an answer such as 'Oh, something pretty … with a nice patio … and a lawn … a rockery, perhaps … and, oh yes, somewhere to grow our own vegetables.' Invite them to put their requirements in the form of a plan and the result is likely to be a muddle bordering on chaos.

But show the same couple a selection of plans or sketches incorporating the desired features and they'll quickly pick one out and say, 'That's it! That's just what we want.'

There you have the idea behind this book: not to try to inform you *how* to design your garden (this, after all, requires a mixture of artistry, skill and knowledge which takes a landscape architect years to acquire) but to offer a choice of garden plans professionally designed to meet the needs of a wide spectrum of home owners.

It's almost too much to expect your particular site to match exactly one of the shapes and sizes shown, or your own list of needs and preferences, but you will find that most of the plans can be adapted to your individual requirements without difficulty. And providing your plot is not *smaller* than the minimum size given, the plan can be usually suited to it.

We have chosen the 22 sets of circumstances most likely to include your own, and there is a design for each. Four of them relate to ASPECT, for this has a telling effect on perhaps the most used feature of the small garden – the patio or sitting-out place. If the aspect at the back of the house is southerly, the patio can then obviously be sited in the best place – as an extension of the home. If the aspect is northerly, there will be no sun unless the leisure area is removed from the immediate vicinity of the house – and the warmth of sunshine is highly desirable, at least in temperate zones like the British Isles. Easterly and westerly aspects need skilful treatment if the most is to be made of them, not only in relation to the sitting-out place, but to the siting of the main planting areas.

A site with a pronounced SLOPE presents problems not easily solved by the amateur. The difficulty is most acute when the incline is directly downwards or directly upwards from the back of the house. Designs No. 5 and No. 6 offer attractive solutions.

Few plots can be accepted as ideal. But some have the fortune to overlook a pleasant VIEW – a bonus which, properly harnessed, will enhance the potential of the garden. Clearly it must be preserved in the best possible way, so that garden and prospect become a single enchanting picture. The other side of the coin is an unsightly or unwanted view – an ugly building, a row of chimney pots and TV aerials, an electricity pylon – which it is desirable to conceal or at least camouflage. Designs No. 7 and No. 8 show ways in which the professional's skill can make the best of either circumstance – the good view and the bad.

Another difficulty that often presents itself is the plot of awkward SHAPE – not necessarily erratically so, but one too narrow, too square, too wedge-shaped to make an agreeable garden simple to design. But it can be done, even to the extent of turning the irregular shape to advantage (see Designs Nos. 9 to 13).

The latter part of the 22 plans is devoted to the special needs of the individual family. The young couple with a new house are faced with the task of making a garden out of the rough, bare, or weed-ridden plot surrounding it – often, these days, a plot that is embarrassingly small. This couple, above all, need help, for they can hardly be expected to have any experience of design, gardening or growing plants. Design No. 14 should help to set them on their way.

But when a FAMILY arrives, the couple's needs are altered. Space must be found for play – a climbing frame, a swing or see-saw and, of course, room for ball games on however small a scale. And that favourite of all toddlers, a sand pit (preferably within sight of Mother in the kitchen) which can be converted later, when it is safe to do so, into an ornamental pool. Planting may be affected, too, with the accent being put on shrubs and grass rather than vulnerable border and bedding plants. Design No. 15 shows how to overcome the problems while preserving an attractive garden.

The business couple with no children who will have little time for gardening outside week-ends (when other leisure pursuits may often take preference) need a garden without frills that makes limited demands. For them we have designed a FORMAL GARDEN (see Design No. 16).

By contrast, the RETIRED COUPLE have a lot more time but, perhaps, less energy. Such couples need a garden in which they can enjoy their leisure, entertain their friends, and also work happily without becoming overtired (Design No. 17).

Inevitably, there are people who delight in the beauty and tranquillity of a garden but look upon its maintenance as a necessary chore rather than a pleasure. For them – but also for those who would like to spend more time gardening but don't have it to spare – the LOW MAINTENANCE garden (Design No. 18) is included.

Then there are the unfortunate ones who love gardens and gardening but suffer from infirmity or old age, and are prevented from carrying out tasks in the normal way. Although, in an ordinary garden, they may be able to do a certain amount of work with specially designed tools, the ideal solution is a garden specifically designed for THE HANDICAPPED (Design No. 19).

There are tens of thousands of gardens around the country crammed with vegetables, and usually some fruit too, all set out in orderly rows. Fine! – nothing matches home-grown produce for flavour and freshness. But can you really call these plots gardens? With careful design, there's no reason why a plot geared to PRODUCTIVITY should not also be an inviting place in which to enjoy one's leisure (Design No. 20).

WATER has enormous fascination in a garden. At rest, it reflects light and mirrors both surrounding planting and the ever-changing sky while providing unending interest with the fish, wildlife, and plants that inhabit or frequent it. In motion, it offers sparkle and music – the perfect accompaniment to the peace of a garden. In more practical terms, water is a real labour-saver – a feature which, once established, needs little or no maintenance. Design No. 21 shows how a delightful garden can be based on the intelligent use of water.

Lastly – even though you may not yet have a SWIMMING POOL – Design No. 22 suggests how a pool can be accommodated without dominating the appearance of the modestly-sized garden to an undesirable degree.

Planning a Garden

If you, or your needs, are not directly accommodated by one of the designs in this book, it is likely that sections or features of one or more will attract you, and you may well be able to compose a design to your liking using them as component parts.

But there will always be some people, with strong creative instincts, who will wish – whether guided or not by our designs – to plan their own garden. And why not? As the work of construction develops and, later, the planting begins to mature, the amateur designer can gain tremendous pleasure – if the plan turns out to be a success. On the other hand, he or she may have to confess to disappointment, if not to complete failure. That's a risk the amateur has to take. For 15 years the Daily Express (of which co-author Donald Farthing has been gardening editor since 1950) ran an annual garden design competition for its readers, excluding professional landscape architects. But the winning design that looked good on paper did not always come up to expectations when laid out as a garden at the Chelsea Show. In that time only a single gold medal was won. When, however, the planning of the Daily Express Chelsea garden was put into the hands of a professional (co-author Guy Farthing)

he quickly achieved a hat-trick of successive gold medals (1977, 1978 and 1979).

Whether you feel capable of designing your own garden or are content to copy or adapt a professional plan, it's still worth learning the basic principles of garden design – if only to give you a better understanding of the thinking behind the various plans in this book.

Just as an architect needs a brief from the client who wants a house built, so the landscape architect or garden designer should begin by knowing what kind of garden is required, including a list of choices and preferences. If you are planning your own garden, you must still have these important facts clear in your mind. What these might be are largely covered by the designs in this book – the needs of newly-weds, business folk, the elderly, the handicapped; the wish for an easily-run garden or a productive one; the desire to solve the problem of a difficult shape or aspect.

The next step is to study the plot – not just for a few minutes, but carefully over a few days. Decide what is worth preserving – a beautiful tree, a stone outcrop, a natural bank, a pleasing view – and what should go. Desirable as most trees are, one must be practical. If a tree is darkening living rooms or depriving an important part of the plot of light, there's no room for sentiment: have it felled. If you have a conscience – and indeed we all should – plant a replacement in a more suitable position: a place where it can be seen and admired at a little distance, or provide shade on a hot summer's day.

Privacy must always be a major consideration. But before you decide to spend a great deal of money on fencing or hedging plants to enclose the whole plot, ask yourself, 'Is it all really necessary?' Do you, for instance, need privacy in the front garden? Would it not be better (not to mention cheaper) to leave the garden open for passers-by to enjoy, to offer a welcome to the approaching visitor?

And is there any real need to fence or hedge in that part of the garden not close to the house? Any sort of screen inevitably causes shade and loss of light to some plants. More than that, it denies the opportunity of vistas or glimpses of the neighbours' gardens, having the effect of extending the boundaries of your own garden. An effective compromise is to plant groups of shrubs, perhaps with an ornamental tree or two, along the boundaries in place of the traditional fence or hedge. A much more natural look is achieved, and the rigid outlines of the plot are no longer obvious. (An example of 'twinned' gardens will be found in Design No. 10.)

If the need to exclude animals – or, in some districts, roving children – makes a screen desirable, it's worth remembering that a living one (a hedge) is cheaper than timber, brick or concrete, and more attractive. Suitable subjects include beech, hornbeam, quickthorn or holly. Many conifers, especially *Cupressocyparis Leylandii*, make a splendid, fast-growing screen, but do not always deter animals.

The next step is to make a list of the features you wish your garden to embrace, heading it with the essential ones. It's a mistake to try to include too many; it is far better to start with a simple canvas and leave the more intricate embroidery till later. Most gardens are designed round a lawn – and this is not surprising, for nothing sets off plants and flowers better, or is more soothing; no surface is more pleasant to sit or lie on. But, in the smallest gardens, a lawn can be difficult to maintain in good condition, and paving stones, gravel, or stone chippings may be a better choice.

Before deciding where to site the patio and the main planting areas, including the vegetables, take into account aspect – the position of the sun at various times of the day. (Designs Nos. 1 to 4 demonstrate the importance of aspect, and offer ways to make the best use of it.)

A garden is only as good as its soil, and the garden planner should be guided by its type. Clay retains moisture – sometimes to the extent of making drainage necessary. Chalk and sand drain rapidly, and 'dry out quickly. The best soil a gardener can wish for is a deep, easily worked loam. But if he is not blessed with it, he need not despair: with the right treatment – the addition of bulky organic matter in quantity – even the poorest soil can be made fertile and the heaviest soil lightened.

Another key consideration is the degree of alkalinity or acidity of the soil, measured by the pH factor. A figure of seven is referred to as neutral – anything below is acid, anything above, alkaline, which means the soil contains lime. Most soils range between pH5 and 8, and you can easily make a check with an inexpensive soil testing

outfit (take samples from various parts of the plot). Some plants have strong objections to lime, which locks up the iron they need: in this bracket are rhododendrons, azaleas, camellias, and summer-flowering heathers, plus a range of other attractive shrubs. Clematises, the carnation family, the brassicas (cabbages, sprouts, etc.), peas and beans flourish best in limey soil.

Acid soils can be brought nearer neutrality by the addition of lime or ground chalk: limey alkaline ones less with the frequent use of sulphate of ammonia and sulphate of iron. But, on the whole, it will be found better to accept the natural character of the soil and plant accordingly. Be guided by what grows well in the district, both in the wild and in neighbouring gardens.

But before anything can be planted, the garden must be planned – without hurry and with care, for it's going to be there a long time. Alterations can be both difficult and costly.

First list the features you have decided upon – patio, lawn, paths, trees, shrubs, flower borders or beds, vegetable plot, play areas and so on. Next take some sheets of plain paper and make some trial sketches – simply plotting in the desired features as blocks or shapes, without any detail. When you achieve an arrangement that appeals to you – keeping in mind the governing factors of size, aspect, surroundings and existing features – try to give it the professional touch. There are tricks which can make an otherwise ordinary, dull garden both attractive and intriguing. It should, for example, have an axis governing the placement of the component areas of the garden.

HOW TALL DOES YOUR GARDEN GROW?

In each garden you will see a key to the type of plants distributed in the garden plan. Three main groups apply; shrubs over 6 ft, shrubs 3–6 ft and ground cover. Here are the key symbols which have been used throughout and an illustration of their height in relation to a 6 ft man.

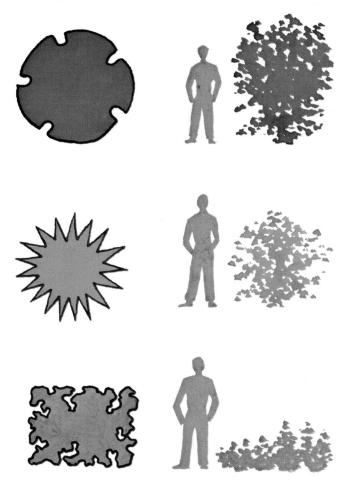

If, as is more often the case than not, the plot is rectangular, it is an advantage to angle the axis, and so negate the rigid shape. Ideally, there should be a focal point – which may well locate itself naturally at the far end of the axis – towards which the eye is led.

Unless a formal garden is planned, in which straight lines and geometrical shapes are acceptable and even desirable, the amateur will usually do best with curves – not fussy ones, but long, flowing, gentle curves.

If the plot is flat, don't accept the fact. Introduce one or more changes of level and you at once achieve an interest and charm that would otherwise be lacking. This need not involve any great amount of earth moving: one has only to remove nine inches of soil from one area, and mound it in another, to create an 18-inch change of level. Often – as when linking two lawns – six inches is enough to bring about the desired effect. The excavation of a pool provides ample soil to create a sizeable rock garden, with interesting slopes, or a bank at the far end of the garden – a feature which, if there is open ground beyond, can create the illusion that the garden has no intervening boundary.

Paths, especially in the small garden, can occupy a significant proportion of the available space – space that could otherwise be usefully employed. So keep them to a minimum, and keep them functional. A path designed purely for access should be as direct as possible; no-one wants a corkscrew route from gate to front door, or a winding one from house to garden shed. But where the path is planned simply for pleasure – as when flanking a flower border, or passing through an area of shrubs – gentle curves are perfectly acceptable. Grass paths, if wide enough, are always attractive. But avoid the common practice of making a stepping stone path across grass. Although you can set the stones low enough to permit the mower to pass over them, the edges call for frequent trimming – a lengthy and tedious job.

Once you have all the details as well as the main points settled you can produce your final plan. Use a sheet of squared graph paper and decide on the appropriate scale. Draw in the boundaries, then the major features – including existing ones, such as trees – and finally the minor features and details.

Then take your plan on to the plot and mark in the key points with pegs, and outline the lawn, beds and borders with strong twine and pegs. A length of garden hose is useful in delineating curves. Now check the proportions and balance of your plan from a good vantage point – an upstairs window is recommended. And finally, check the positioning of trees, paths and structures (such as greenhouse, screens or pergola) from both living room windows and patio – the places from which the garden will be most often viewed. When – and only when – you are completely satisfied that nothing can be improved, you can set about building your garden.

The setting-out plans show the radial points where pegs should be sited to describe arcs for the curves.

1 Garden Facing South

A south-facing plot is, of course, the sunniest of all, and the owner should make the most of his good fortune. A successful example (shown here) is a Daily Express garden which won a gold medal at Chelsea. The design makes fullest use of the southerly aspect, while the skilful use of curves and subtle changes of level produce a result that is restful yet stimulating.

The generous patio – an extension of the domestic living space – looks out over a large pool (so cooling on a hot day) to a lawn which sweeps up the garden to an arresting feature, a timber arbour shaded by climbing plants. This is one of three places from which the garden can be viewed and enjoyed in comfort, the others being the patio with its attendant roses and flower-filled urns, and the wooden bench opposite the pool. This is sheltered by ornamental trees and shrubs which have another important function – to conceal the greenhouse and the kitchen garden, an easily accessible, slightly raised, plot which lends itself to intensive cultivation.

We mentioned changes of level ... the lawn is slightly dished along the greater length of its spine, and falls away into the longer grass bordering the pool. The path leading to the greenhouse area rises up shallow steps, causing the island shrub bed to incline upwards to the general slightly elevated level of the rear of the garden.

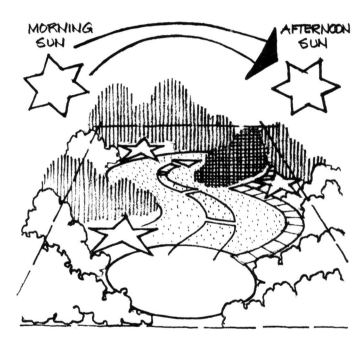

How the sun moves across the garden, always favouring the house and patio. Stars show the balanced focal points whilst the undulating arrow shows the main path of vision.

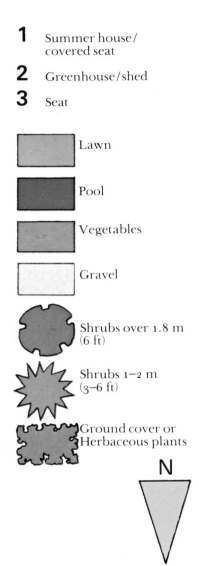

1 Summer house/
covered seat

2 Greenhouse/shed

3 Seat

Lawn

Pool

Vegetables

Gravel

Shrubs over 1.8 m
(6 ft)

Shrubs 1–2 m
(3–6 ft)

Ground cover or
Herbaceous plants

N

*The plan shows how the chosen
features have been carefully
balanced around the S-shaped
lawn, and how the regular lines of
the plot have been concealed.*

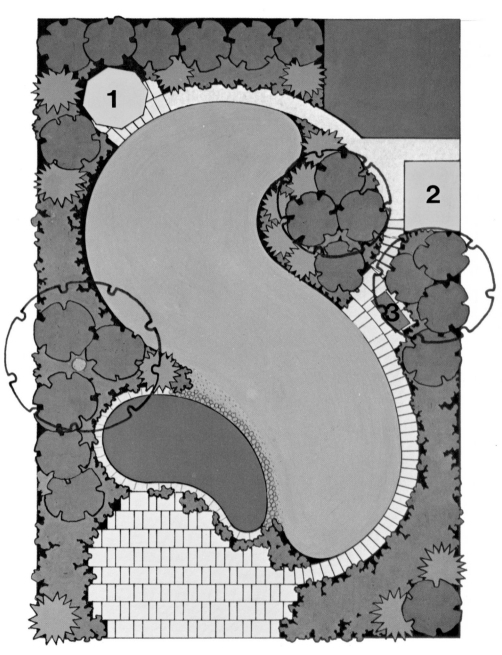

This design shares its sunny warmth with a cool sophistication that meets the needs of the house owner with a modern outlook.

This garden is a clear example of the way in which the severe lines of the average suburban garden can be effectively disguised – a skill which, as can be proved all too often, is lacking in almost every garden laid out by its owner.

The perspective – seen as if from a window of the house – reveals the graceful, curving lines of this sun-filled garden. Yet there is coolness, too – provided by the water of the pool, reflecting the planting beyond and the passing clouds, and by the background trees, giving shade for the summerhouse.

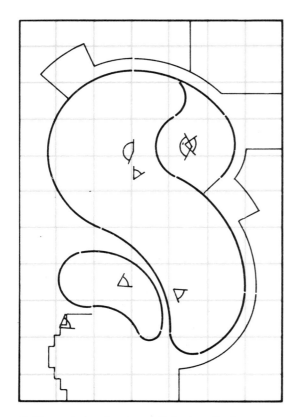

Setting-out plan showing radial points. Each square represents 2 × 2 m.

Pool edge – where a soft edge between water and lawn is required:

Excavate the pool area to a depth of 45–60 cm (18–24 in.) Lay a butyl liner on 25–50 mm (1–2 in.) of sand, tucking the edges over as shown in the sketch.

Spread a 1:6 cement/sand mortar bed from the edge of the lawn over the liner and set cobbles into the mortar before it sets.

Use Silglaze to neutralise any lime and to bring out the colour of the cobbles.

Size of liner required, regardless of the shape or depth of the pool, is worked out like this:

Length of liner – Overall length of the pool plus twice the maximum depth, plus 20.5 cm (8 in.) for overlap.

Width of liner – Overall width of the pool plus twice the maximum depth, plus 20.5 cm (8 in.) for overlap.

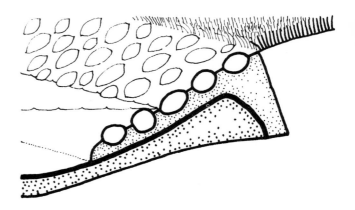

For pool edge against paving, see Garden 2 (page 22).

2 Garden Facing West

If a southerly aspect is the most desirable for a garden, with maximum sunshine benefiting both house occupants and plants, a westerly one has much in its favour. The heat of the noonday sun does not fall directly on the house, yet plenty is available at that part of the day – afternoon and evening – when leisure hours are most usually available.

The patio sited in the right-hand corner of our west-facing garden in fact receives sun from midday, or even earlier, till sunset or close to it – and at any time of the year. A pool overlooked by a small tree at the far end lends coolness to this suntrap.

A feature of the garden is that all is not unfolded at a glance. Sit on the patio and the curving path draws the eye through some solid shrub planting ... hiding what? (It happens to be the greenhouse and vegetable areas.) Let the gaze wander further up the garden and it is interrupted by the shrubs forming the backcloth to the pool. A walk up the path reveals the upper lawn and its surrounding planting – the top half of the figure eight which forms the basis of the design. In the far corner is another ornamental tree – the focal point terminating the line of vision from the kitchen (from which, as the housewife well knows, the garden is most frequently seen by her).

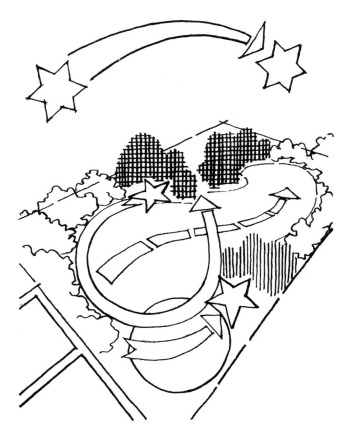

How the sun moves, always favouring the patio. Stars show the opposing focal points; arrows show the main paths of vision.

1 Greenhouse

2 Statue/Birdbath

3 Patio

 Lawn

 Vegetables

 Pool

 Gravel

 Shrubs over 1.8 m (6 ft)

 Shrubs 1–2 m (3–6 ft)

 Ground cover or Herbaceous plants

N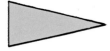

The plan shows the twin axes – the first, from the supposed kitchen window (bottom left), takes the eye the length of the garden; the second, originating from the patio outside the lounge (bottom right) where most sun can be enjoyed, gives a view across the lawn to a stone ornament.

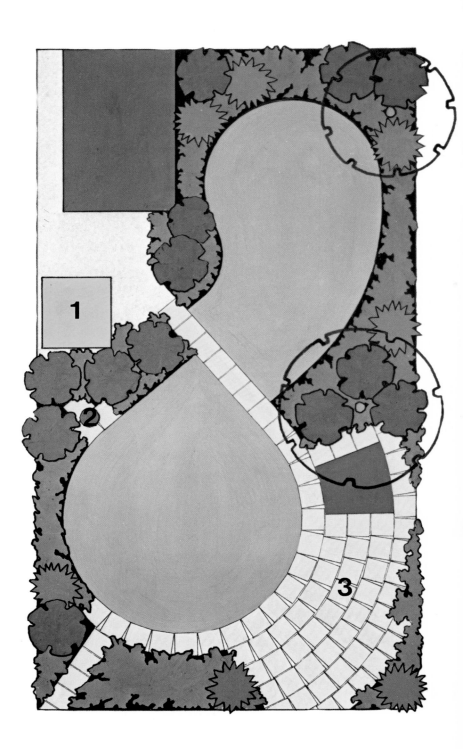

Curves soften the rectangular outlines of the plot, and the best visual use is made of its length by siting the vegetable plot to the side, rather than at the end of the garden. To give additional interest, the far lawn could be elevated by six inches, in which case the path should be gradually raised to this level as it approaches the junction of the two lawns.

The vista from the house windows at once poses the question: 'Just how big is this garden – where does it end?' The illusion of infinite depth is fostered by the introduction of a second lawn, forming a narrow waistline, cinched in by tall, dense planting. The ornamental tree and shrubs on the right are mirrored by the small pool, while those on the left embrace the statue or bird bath as a focal point.

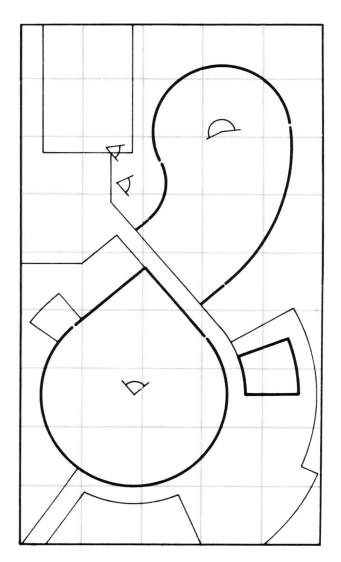

Setting-out plan showing radial points. Each square represents 2 × 2 m.

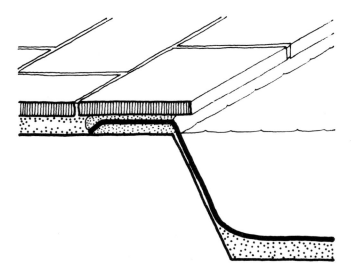

Pool edge – where pool borders path or patio:

Excavate the pool area, lay a butyl liner on sand, and bed the overlap in a 1:6 cement/sand mortar mix.

Bed the paving slabs immediately surrounding the pool on 1:8 cement/sand mortar, allowing an overhang of approximately 5 cm (2 in.). Ensure that the whole of the edging is level, using a spirit level on a length of straight board.

3 Garden Facing East

shrubs, with colourful herbaceous subjects in the middle of the garden, directly facing the patio. It is important to include a substantial number of evergreens, not only for winter interest but for

It may be pleasant to walk out on to a patio bathed in morning sunshine, but few of us have time to spend on leisure at the beginning of the day. What we need is a sitting-out place favoured with sun from, say, noon till evening. And, in the east-facing garden, that means siting the patio on the north (south-facing) side so that it collects maximum sun. In our design, this is reached either from the living room (on right) or kitchen (on left). A small ornamental tree on the far side of the patio gives shade in the summer months at the hottest time of the day, while attendant low-growing shrubs or flower filled tubs are sufficient to break the prevailing south-west wind. This sitting-out place is far enough away from the house to catch the evening sun.

The basis of the design is a simple, kidney-shaped lawn giving both space and interest. It is partly encircled by a path of square paving stones that 'grows' out of the patio and finally arrives at the focal point – a statue or a stone seat.

The utility area is at the rear of the garden, well concealed by a screen of shrubs. Those on the north side, plus the tree, hide the shed. The greenhouse is optional; the owner may prefer to devote the space to extra vegetables or soft fruit.

The planting relies mainly on well-chosen

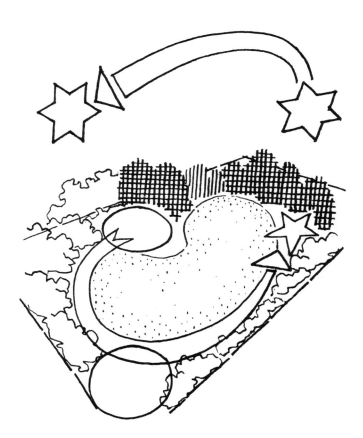

The patio is sited to gather the sun in the latter part of the day. From here the path sweeps round to a focal point.

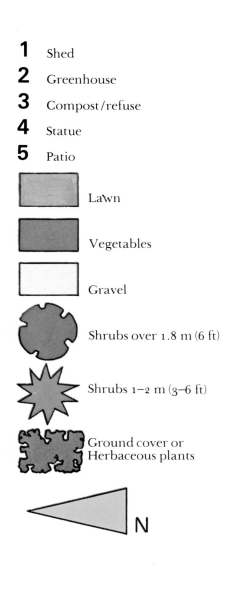

1 Shed
2 Greenhouse
3 Compost/refuse
4 Statue
5 Patio

Lawn

Vegetables

Gravel

Shrubs over 1.8 m (6 ft)

Shrubs 1–2 m (3–6 ft)

Ground cover or
Herbaceous plants

N

*This is a simple garden to lay out. Fix the
outline of the lawn and the rest – path, paved
areas, shrub and herbaceous borders – falls
into place. The well-screened rear (productive)
area can be organised as desired.*

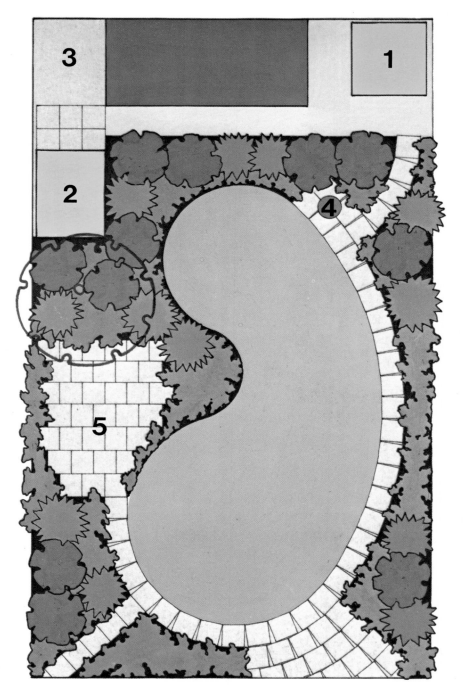

their foliage. Climbers – roses, clematises, or a wisteria – should back the patio. The small planting area beneath the kitchen windows could be filled with roses or scented herbs.

The garden is ideally suited to a medium sized plot of about 18 metres by 11 metres (60 by 35 feet). Any extra length can be utilised for vegetables or even a small orchard.

The patio has the advantage of not only receiving the afternoon and evening sun, but of giving shelter from cold east or north winds. The significance of the small statue as a focal point (when viewed from the house) is clearly seen. And yet again, the curving lawn, disappearing round a mid-distance prominence, leaves the visitor intrigued by what – and how much – lies beyond.

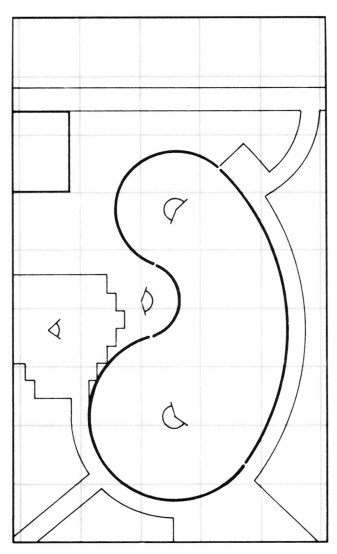

Setting-out plan showing radial points. Each square represents 2 × 2 m.

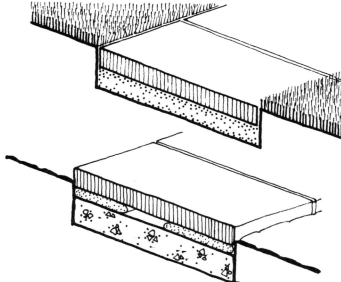

Paving – Where a path has turf on both sides:

Lay the paving slabs on a 5 cm (2 in.) bed of sand with four dabs of mortar. Using a spirit level, tap level with a wooden mallet. The joints should be mortared in to ensure that the sand bed is protected. The surface of the slabs should be below the level of the turf to facilitate mowing.

Where a path has a bed or border on one or both sides, or where the ground has been built up or is unstable:

Lay a bed of 7.5–10 cm (3–4 in.) of concrete (1 part cement, 2 parts sand, 4 parts aggregate). Bed the paving slabs on 1:6 mortar. The joints need nor be mortared.

4 Garden Facing North

For every house that happily faces south at the back, there's one that faces north. But that need cause the owner no heartache. It simply means that the leisure area is moved out into the sun. In our suggested design, it is sited to the right, so that one can bask in the sunshine (when available!) all day long and receive the last lingering rays when the sun sinks, facing you, in the west.

This garden shows that straight lines and rectangular shapes are no hindrance to a pleasing design if carefully used. The paving (all square slabs, easily laid) is nicely balanced by the two L-shaped lawns and their attendant borders of shrubs, roses, herbaceous plants and – if you wish – bedding plants or annuals. The first lawn spreads itself like a carpet before the living room and, with its shade and nearby pool, provides a cool place to enjoy in the warmest days of summer.

A pair of offset plant barriers – for that is what they are – conceal enough of the upper part of the garden to make it interesting (note the steps up from the patio – creating a slight, but important, change of level). Room has been found for a built-in barbecue – almost an essential piece of outdoor-living equipment these days.

Hidden from both the patio and the lower lawn is an area that can be used as the owner wishes – for vegetables, for fruit (the shape is convenient for a netted cage) or, if there are children, for play equipment.

The elevation demonstrates the rewarding effects of a simple change of level. The raised upper lawn, approached by two steps, automatically 'dishes' the lower one and creates slightly banked flower borders.

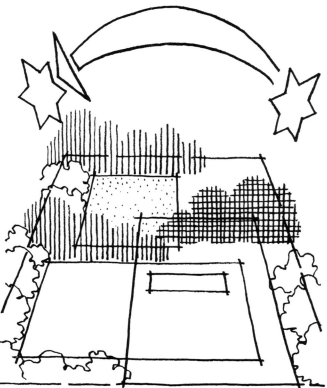

No sun reaches the back of the house, so the leisure area is moved out, but is still easily accessible.

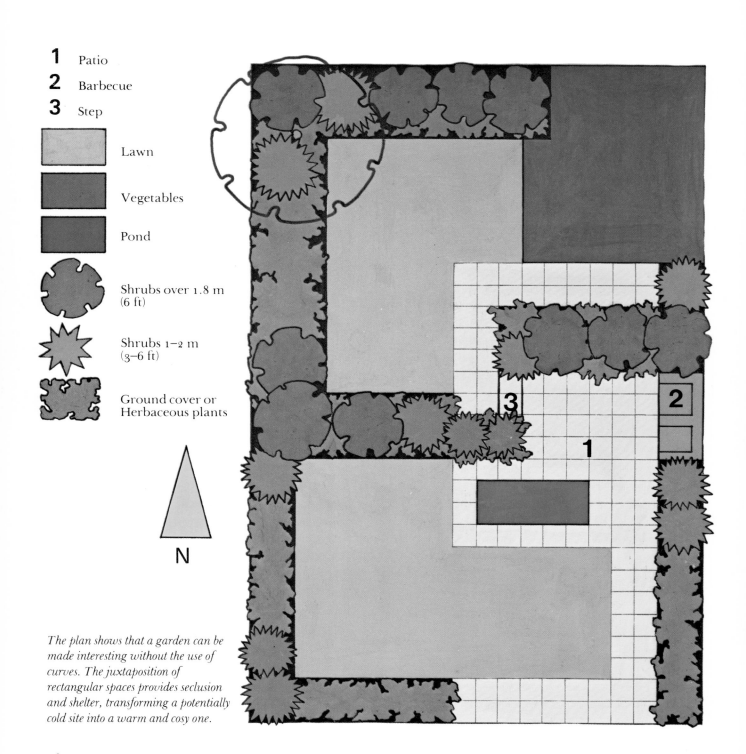

1 Patio
2 Barbecue
3 Step

Lawn

Vegetables

Pond

Shrubs over 1.8 m
(6 ft)

Shrubs 1–2 m
(3–6 ft)

Ground cover or
Herbaceous plants

N

The plan shows that a garden can be made interesting without the use of curves. The juxtaposition of rectangular spaces provides seclusion and shelter, transforming a potentially cold site into a warm and cosy one.

Although perhaps too formal for a rural setting, this simple design is ideally suited to the small suburban or town site.

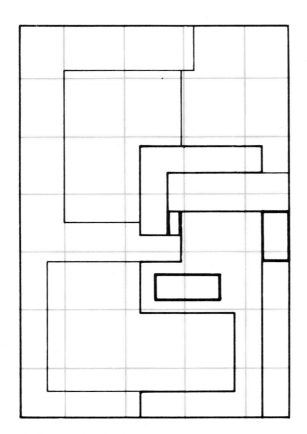

Setting-out plan. Each square represents 2 × 2 m.

Barbecue – with store for logs and charcoal:

Use a well-baked stock brick (your local builder's merchant will advise). Overall size:

60 × 194 × 90 cm (2 ft × 6 ft 4 in. × 3 ft).

Foundations: Dig trenches 30 cm (1 ft) wide and 25 cm (10 in.) deep, and fill with concrete to within 7.5 cm (3 in.) below ground level.

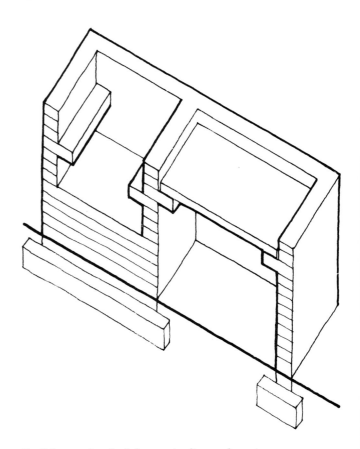

Build up the bricks as indicated, using a mortar mix of 2 parts cement, 1 part hydrated lime, 10 parts sand.

The drawing shows a paving slab 90 × 45 cm (3 ft × 1 ft 6 in.) supported by bricks built into the wall. Similar supports are shown for the grille which can be made by a local blacksmith or ironworker.

5 Garden Sloping Away from the House

A house with a garden that slopes away from it is a house with a view, distant or limited. This gives the opportunity to design the garden as an integral part of that view. As with the garden that rises away from the house, the slope should be put to work to produce compelling and intriguing effects.

In our plan for this situation, the fall of the site is harnessed to allow water to tumble from an upper pool into a second and then a third pool, all three of which are overlooked by the patio, and intersected by a winding staircase that leads down to and around a level, curved lawn. Further steps approach an area of longer grass in which fruit trees are planted; while on the right a ramp gives access to shed and vegetable plot, well guarded by closely planted shrubs.

This is a garden of pleasantly informal character. The upper (nearer) part simulates an alpine scene, with rocks buttressing the patio area and bordering the pools. Full use is made of alpine plants and conifers, particularly those of a conical or fastigiate nature. Rocks in the less steep gradients are interspersed with small areas of scree (gravel or stone chippings), with procumbent and trailing plants. Think, if you like, of a miniature mountainside flowing down to a more fertile lower region, where growth is more luxurious – and there you have the key to the planting backing the lawn, and providing the link with that view beyond.

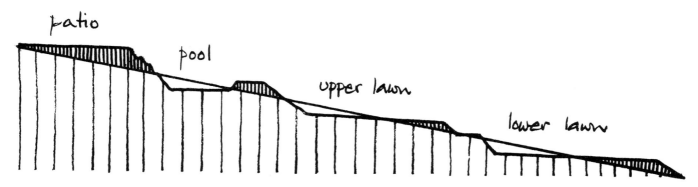

The sectional drawing shows how the steep gradient is transformed into four distinct, level areas – each with a character of its own. The opportunities for creating attractive rock slopes are obvious.

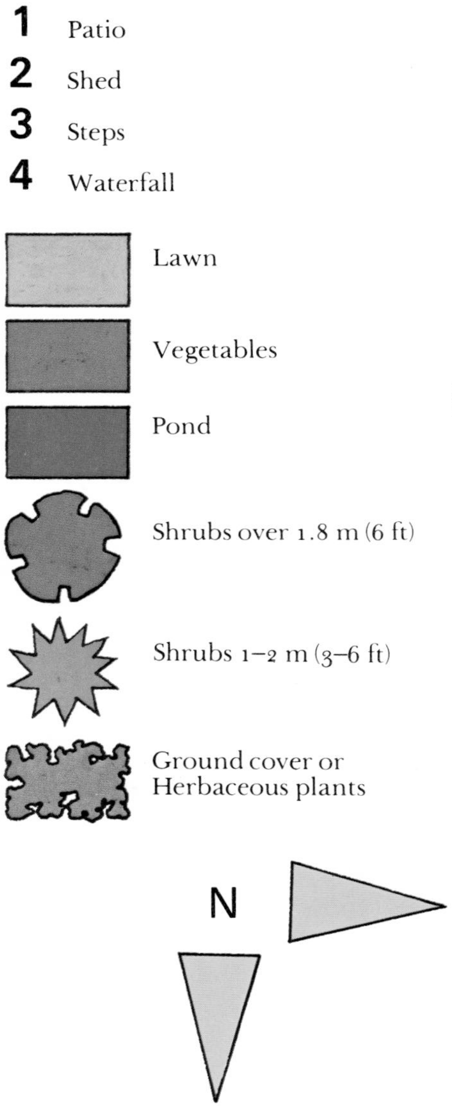

1 Patio
2 Shed
3 Steps
4 Waterfall

Lawn

Vegetables

Pond

Shrubs over 1.8 m (6 ft)

Shrubs 1–2 m (3–6 ft)

Ground cover or
Herbaceous plants

N

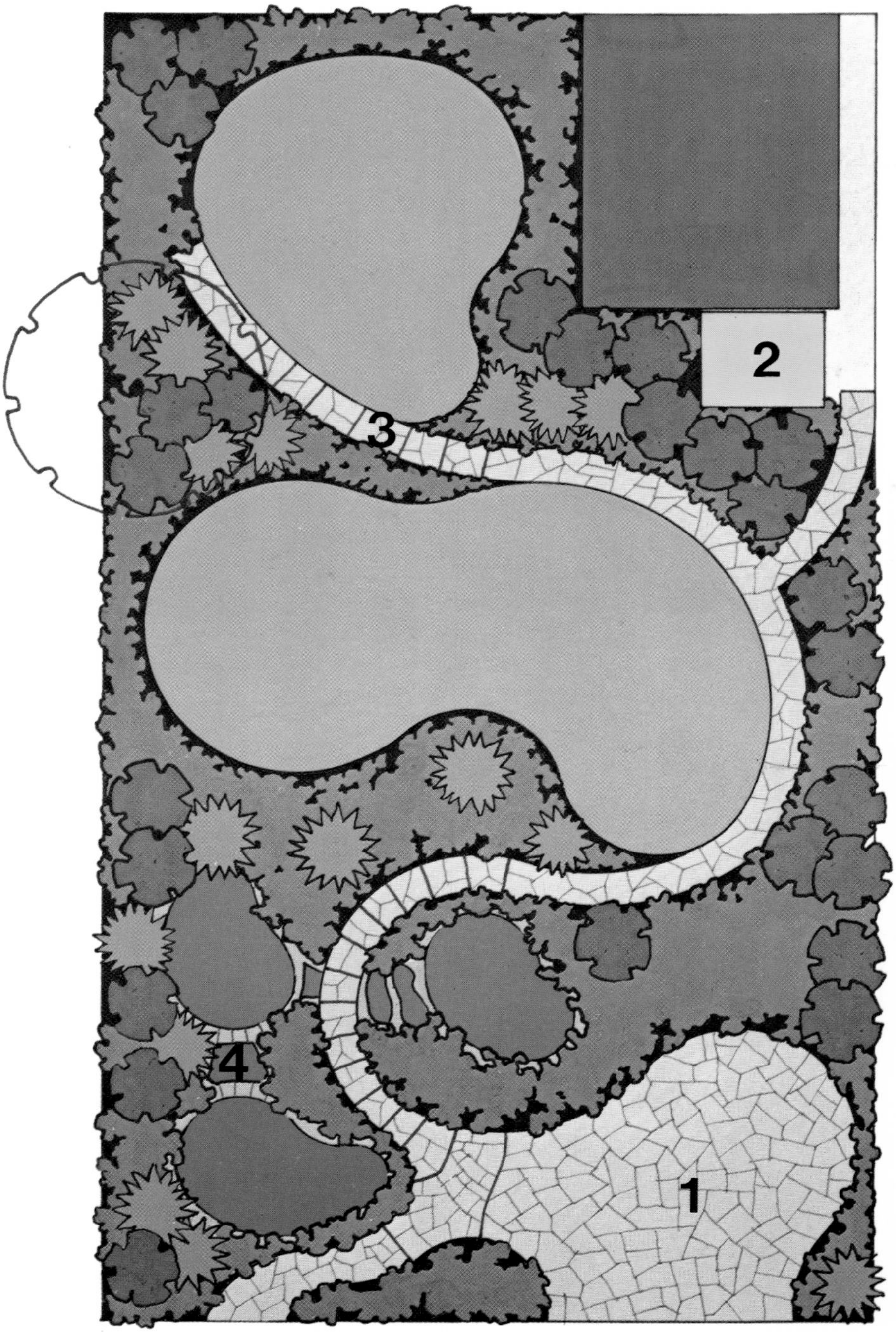

A plan (vertical view) is necessary for the
laying-out of any garden, so that the various
features can be accurately defined. But, in this
case, the plan gives an impression very
different from that of the elevation view on the
next page. Here you can see only the curved
shapes – the snaking path, the trio of pools, the
curved lawns.

Now you see how the garden is designed to make use of the descending slope, affording an unhindered view – just as one might enjoy it from a hilltop. From the patio the path runs down through the pools and among irregular rocks to what might be an alpine lawn. Beyond, only the upper parts of the trees and shrubs are seen, once again creating that sense of mystery that it so important in a garden, whatever its type.

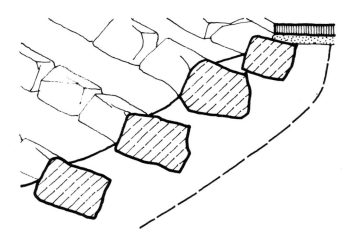

Rock Garden: It is important to lay the rocks as rows of steps, not haphazardly, to simulate natural strata or outcrops.

Individual rocks should be placed so that the top surface slopes back slightly into the hill or mound, to collect rainwater and also to prevent erosion of top soil.

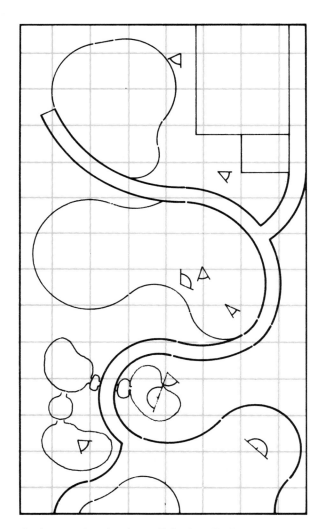

Setting-out plan showing radial points. Each square represents 2 × 2 m.

6 Garden Sloping Towards the House

A site rising away from the back of the house is always regarded as 'difficult'. But with thought and careful planning the apparent disadvantages can become of value. The slope, for example, allows water to cascade from the upper pool into the lower ones, making a delightful feature for the two-level patio area. The wall retaining the lowest pool, and the steps, provide useful seating for guests at a summer party. The lawn above the upper pool is approached by further steps and, with its surrounding planting, supplies a pleasant area for relaxation. A diagonal ramp invites exploration of what lies beyond. This turns out to be the productive part of the garden – vegetables and fruit – with an attendant shed, well hidden behind a bold group of shrubs. The mower, as well as other tools, will need to be kept in this shed because it affords easiest access to the lawn (hence the ramp, and not steps).

The planting of a sloping site has to be done with care. Besides the visual considerations, the possibility of soil washing away must always be kept in mind, and if any gradient is at all steep, some minor terracing – perhaps with a few large stones or logs – may be necessary. Ground cover is invaluable as a stabilising agent and should be used extensively.

In our design, two trees, supported by shrubs, form the basis of the planting. The borders on each side of the garden can be planted as the owner wishes – with shrubs, roses, or herbaceous subjects or, perhaps most happily, with a mixture of all three. The beds attending the pools offer opportunities for introducing aquatic and trailing plants, with alpines in the drier areas.

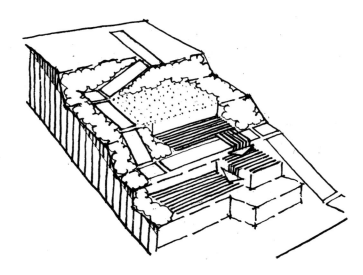

The sketch shows in diagrammatic form how the inward-facing slope is organised into terraces linked by ramps and steps

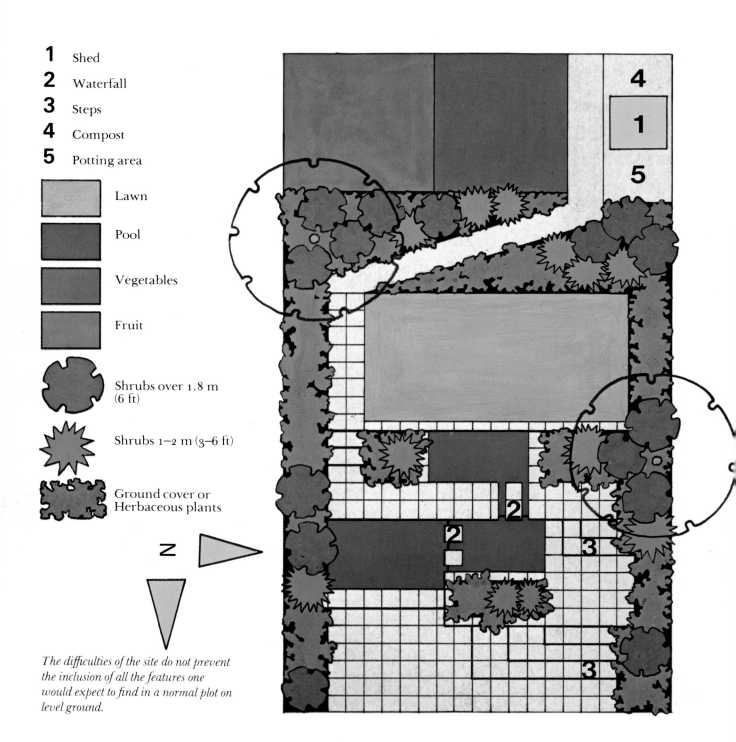

1 Shed
2 Waterfall
3 Steps
4 Compost
5 Potting area

Lawn

Pool

Vegetables

Fruit

Shrubs over 1.8 m
(6 ft)

Shrubs 1–2 m (3–6 ft)

Ground cover or
Herbaceous plants

N

*The difficulties of the site do not prevent
the inclusion of all the features one
would expect to find in a normal plot on
level ground.*

Paving – almost an essential adjunct of formal ornamental pools – plays an important part in this garden. The frequent changing of levels and the attendant planting combine to give it additional attraction.

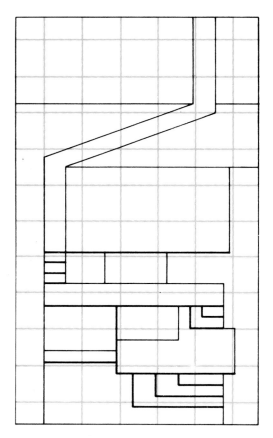

Setting-out plan. Each square represents 2 × 2 m.

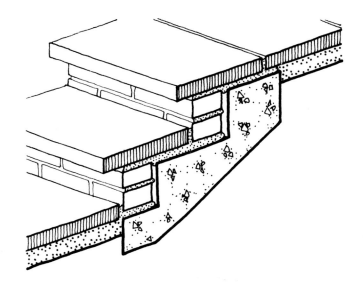

Steps: Form a concrete base for the steps with 15 cm (6 in.) risers and with treads the width of the paving slab minus 5 cm (2 in.).

Lay two courses of bricks and bed the paving slab on a cement/sand mortar bed allowing 4 cm (1½ in.) overhang.

7 Garden to Screen an Eyesore

Unless you live in the country, there's always the chance of an eyesore, or at least an unwelcome view, obtruding on the garden. Or maybe you don't want to be overlooked from the windows of a house on an opposing plot. A screen of trees is the obvious long-term solution, but trees need time to grow and something more immediate is required from the garden design. The one we show tackles the problem boldly with a 2.7 metre (eight-foot) wall (it could well be less: the actual height needed can be determined by trial and error, using a long cane, or perhaps a ladder). The

wall itself is in no way an eyesore – as it might be if it stood on its own, since it forms the back of a pergola-covered patio area and is softened by climbing plants (also used along the boundary wall or fence). A pool, conforming with the rectangular pattern of the garden, completes an interesting leisure area, which faces a neat lawn backed by shrubs. A sundial, or statue, gives character to the far end of the garden, mainly occupied by a second lawn, useful as a play area for children (alternatively the ground could be used for vegetables or fruit). At the very back is the long-term screen – most quickly achieved by the conifer *Cupressocyparis Leylandii*, which can put on a metre (three feet) a year once it is established.

Use is made of the screening wall to hide the lean-to shed or greenhouse (if greenhouse, the two large bushes on the far side would be omitted, to allow maximum light).

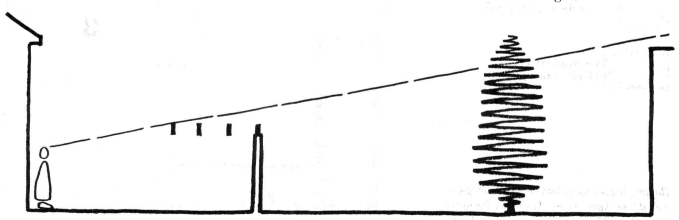

The wall, backing the pergola, does the main job of screening the eyesore – immediately. In later years, conifers at the rear of the garden will round off the strategy.

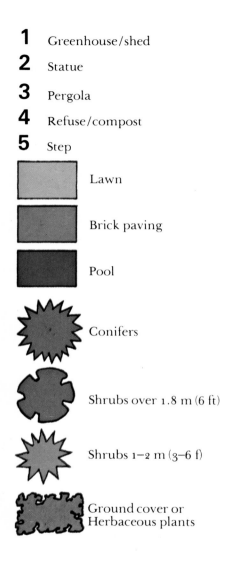

1 Greenhouse/shed
2 Statue
3 Pergola
4 Refuse/compost
5 Step

Lawn

Brick paving

Pool

Conifers

Shrubs over 1.8 m (6 ft)

Shrubs 1–2 m (3–6 f)

Ground cover or
Herbaceous plants

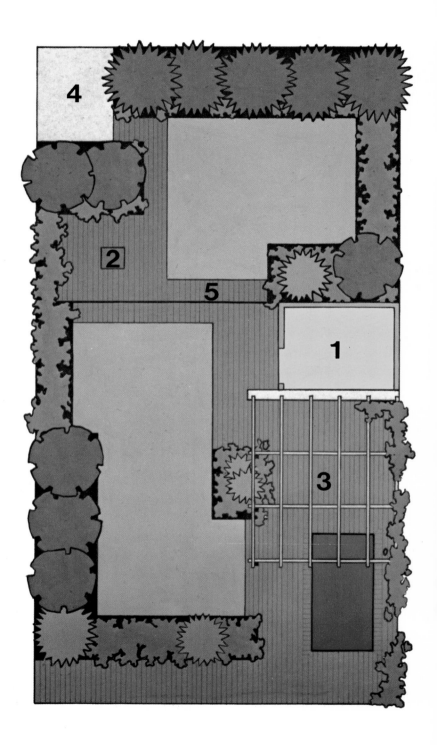

*Balance is a necessary part of garden design –
and it is not lacking here. The major feature of
the high wall is counter-weighted by the long
lawn on the left and the paved area with its
focal point of a stone sundial or statue.*

The paving chosen is a warm brick – specially hard paving bricks must be used.

The perspective view gives conclusive proof of the efficacy of the screening operation. As soon as the wall-backed pergola is built, the owners have a secluded leisure area in which to relax and forget the offending eyesore.

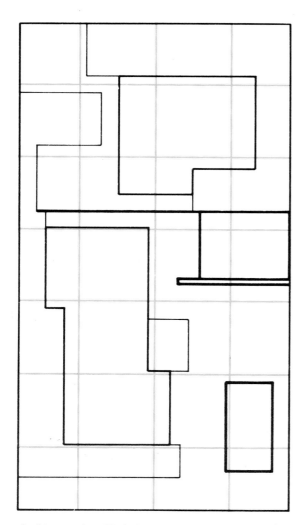

Setting-out plan. Each square represents 2 × 2 m.

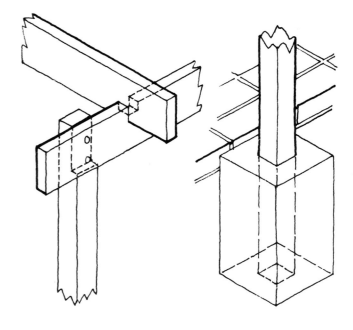

Columns: Dig holes 22 × 22 × 50 cm (9 × 9 × 20 in.) deep. Place a 7.5 cm (3 in.) square timber post in each hole, backfilling with concrete. Cut 2.5 cm (1 in.) notches in the tops of the columns to take the horizontal members.

Horizontal members: Screw three 15 × 5 cm (6 × 2 in.) joists to the top of the columns. Cut notches 2.5 × 4 cm (1 × 1½ in.) wide in the tops of the joists and in the bottom of the cross members at the points of intersection. Fix the six 15 × 4 cm (6 × 1½ in.) cross members to the joists. Apply two coats of perservative stain to all timbers.

8 Garden with a View

... by which we mean, of course, a desirable view. If you are lucky enough to have this valuable asset to your property, everything possible must be done not only to perserve it, but to create a gracious setting for it – just as one would seek to find the perfect frame for a work of art. It is patently necessary to leave the end of the garden open. But equally, because the view will most commonly be enjoyed from the rear windows of the house and its adjoining patio, the planting must be planned with care, and thought for the eventual spread of ornamental trees and shrubs. The ideal arrangement is to confine tall-growing subjects to the side boundaries, with medium and short-growers sloping towards the centre – as our central group on the right and the opposing group towards the rear demonstrate.

The major part of this uncluttered, easily run garden is, not surprisingly, taken up with the two interestingly shaped lawns, whose smooth green swards make the perfect foreground for the distant view. The effect of this is enhanced by the raising of the terrace.

The long path, originating from the patio, invites a stroll towards the view and, by its winding nature, seems to unite the garden with it. A pleasing prospect merits more than one viewpoint, and the secluded, sheltered seat offers a delightful vista.

Crazy paving, less popular these days, has been chosen for this garden because its informality suits the flowing lines. It must be laid well and smoothly, using warm, subdued colours.

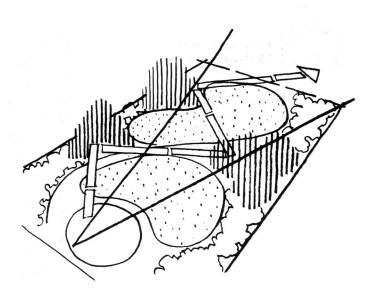

The sketch shows how the view from the raised terrace is framed by the planting each side of the garden. The foreshortening that would result from an unbroken lawn is avoided by creating two lawns of different size and shape, dividing them with a winding path, and leading the eye to the view by a slower, less direct route.

1 Shed

2 Compost

3 Bench

4 Step

 Lawn

Random paving

 Shrubs over 1.8 m (6 ft)

 Shrubs 1–2 m (3–6 ft)

 Ground cover or Herbaceous plants

N

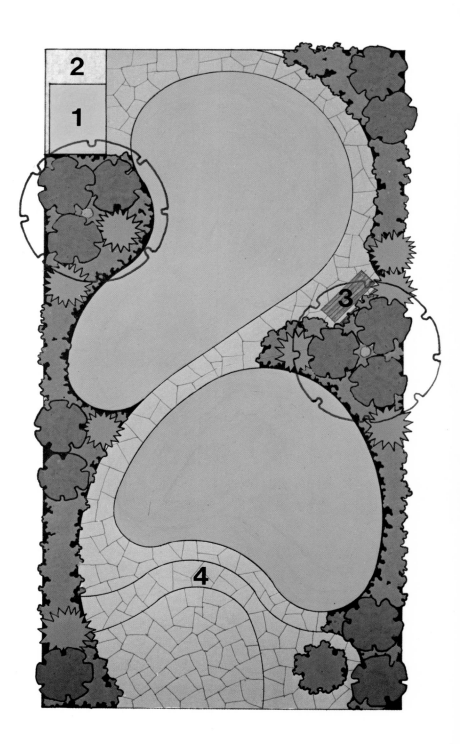

The two opposing trees are not sited solely to help frame the view. The one on the right provides shade for a seat facing across the further lawn; the tree on the left conceals the shed or greenhouse beyond it.

Where does this garden end? That's the question the designer – and, in due course, the owner – wants the visitor to ask. It was the same question Capability Brown loved to pose, and one of the tricks that he used to persuade guests in the big house that the host's estate extended far into the distance was the ha-ha, a deep hidden ditch separating the garden from the fields – and cattle – beyond. An invisible boundary is still desirable in the modern garden with a view – and the deep, wide ditch may yet be a useful way of deterring unwanted visitors, while preserving the uninterrupted view. As an alternative, we suggest the small-mesh material sold for garden windbreaks which is almost invisible at a distance.

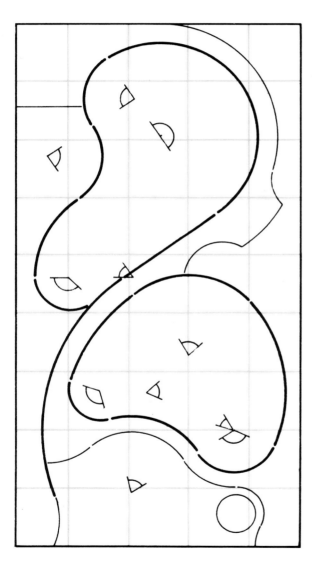

Setting-out plan showing radial points. Each square represents 2 × 2 m.

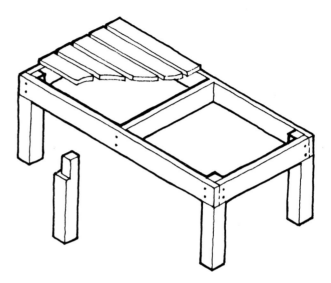

Garden bench: Height 120 × 60 × 45 cm (4 ft × 2 ft × 18 in.) high.

Legs: 7.5 × 7.5 cm (3 × 3 in.) by 45 cm (18 in.). Cut out 2 × 8.5 cm ($\frac{3}{4}$ × 3$\frac{1}{2}$ in.) pieces on two sides.

Seat frame: Two 10 × 2.5 × 120 cm (4 in. × 1 in × 4 ft) members. Three 10 × 2.5 × 55 cm (4 in. × 1 in. × 1 ft 10 in.) members.

Slats: Six 7.5 × 2 × 120 cm (3 in. × $\frac{3}{4}$ in. × 4 ft) slats.

Before assembly, apply two coats of preservative stain, which can be obtained from any timber supplier, to all timber. Ask for 'planed soft wood'.

Use 5 cm (2 in.) long brass or non-ferrous screws to assemble legs and frame, and 4 cm (1$\frac{1}{2}$ in.) screws for the slats.

9 Long, Narrow Garden

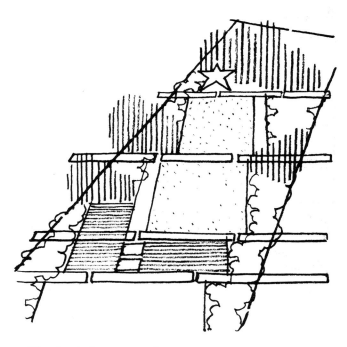

Before the 1939–45 war, houses were commonly built on long, narrow plots, and it is rare to find such a garden well designed. The first essential is to break up the plot into sections to reduce its length to the eye. The next is to defeat the constriction of the closely parallel boundaries by off-setting the axis. A glance at the plan shows how this can be achieved.

The square-paved patio is separated from the garden beyond by two rectangular pools. Cross these to begin the interesting walk past the twin lawns and the neighbouring triangular borders. The perspective view shows how these cunningly conceal what lies beyond at each stage, the final barrier guarding what turns out to be the real end of the garden – the tool shed and vegetable plots.

It will, of course, take several years for the trees and shrubs to reach the stage of maturity that makes the ultimate effect possible. But the garden can be made very attractive in the intervening years by planting herbaceous plants and annuals, including taller growing kinds like mallows and sweet peas (in clumps) between the young shrubs.

Although the garden is shown in a rural setting, it can be equally effective in suburb or town.

The sketch demonstrates how the long plot is broken up into interlinking sections – each one a stepping-stone to the next, and culminating in a focal point at the end of the off-set axis.

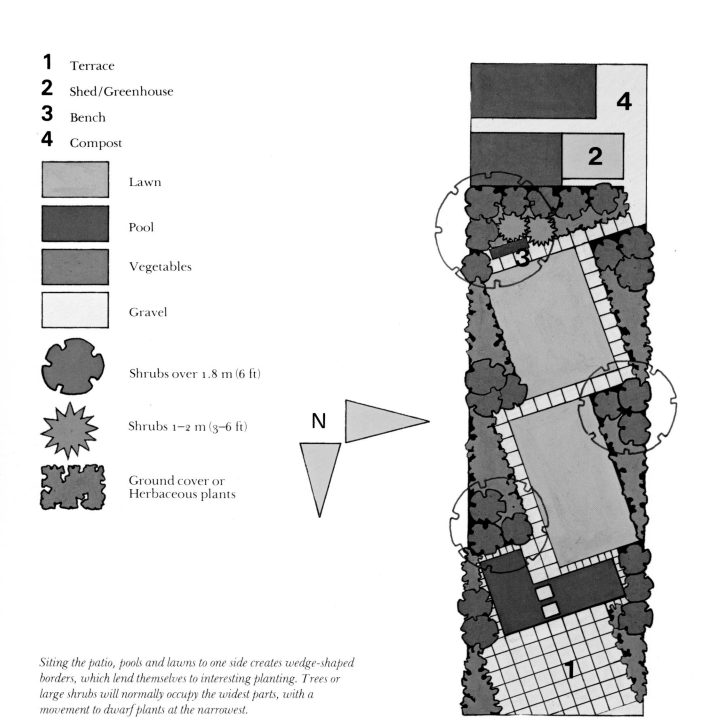

1 Terrace
2 Shed/Greenhouse
3 Bench
4 Compost

Lawn

Pool

Vegetables

Gravel

Shrubs over 1.8 m (6 ft)

Shrubs 1–2 m (3–6 ft)

Ground cover or
Herbaceous plants

N

*Siting the patio, pools and lawns to one side creates wedge-shaped
borders, which lend themselves to interesting planting. Trees or
large shrubs will normally occupy the widest parts, with a
movement to dwarf plants at the narrowest.*

Looking at this garden from the patio, it is hard to realise that it is confined by a long, narrow plot. Compare it with the dreary, unimaginative gardens one so often sees – long, thin lawn, bounded by a thin, straight path and strap-like borders following the line of the fences.

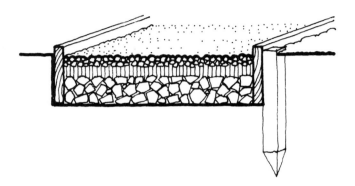

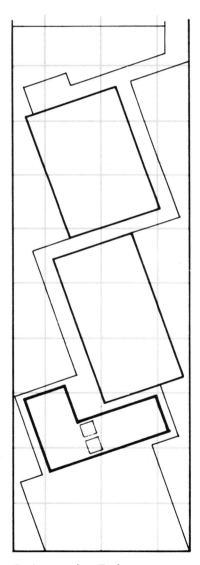

Setting-out plan. Each square represents 2 × 2 m.

Gravel path: Dig out the topsoil to a depth of 12.5 cm (5 in.). Treat 15 × 2.5 cm (6 × 1 in.) edging boards with preservative and fix them to 4 × 4 × 38 cm (1½ × 1½ × 15 in.) long pegs driven into the ground.

Lay 7.5 cm (3 in.) of hardcore (broken stones, brickbats, etc.) and consolidate.

Lay and roll approximately 3 cm (1 in.) of hoggin (small pebbles bound with clay). Roll into the hoggin about 2.5 cm (1 in.) of 6 mm (¼ in.) gravel.

10 The 'Twinned' Garden

Small plots are today the rule rather than the exception when new dwellings are built – so small, in fact, that owners used to more space may feel claustrophobic and shut in. There is a simple solution, if a pair of neighbours can agree: the 'twinning' of their gardens. Each will want to preserve some privacy, but this need not involve a barrier down the length of their common boundary; a wall or fence a third of the way down, to ensure that the patio area is not overlooked, is usually sufficient – as is shown in our design (in this, a brick wall is employed). Beyond that, the boundary is delineated only by an area of rough grass between the gardens' lawns – an area enlivened in spring by daffodils and other bulbs. The planting is deliberately kept low to allow the eye to travel on into the neighbouring garden, giving the impression that each of the gardens extends much farther than in fact it does, the benefit being mutual.

The left-hand garden has an interesting sequence of slightly raised beds abutting the wall, the last one rounding the end of the wall to form a link with the adjoining garden. The patio of the right-hand garden is dominated by a pool of generous size, crossed by a bridge. Both patios have crazy paving which is carried on into the paths bounding the lawns. The surrounding planting is similar – mainly shrubs, roses and herbaceous subjects, some of which serve to screen the vegetable plots at the rear.

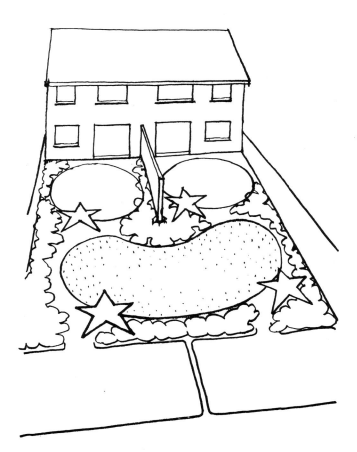

Two semi-detached houses, each with its garden and its privacy – but with TWICE the normal view, DOUBLE the feeling of space.

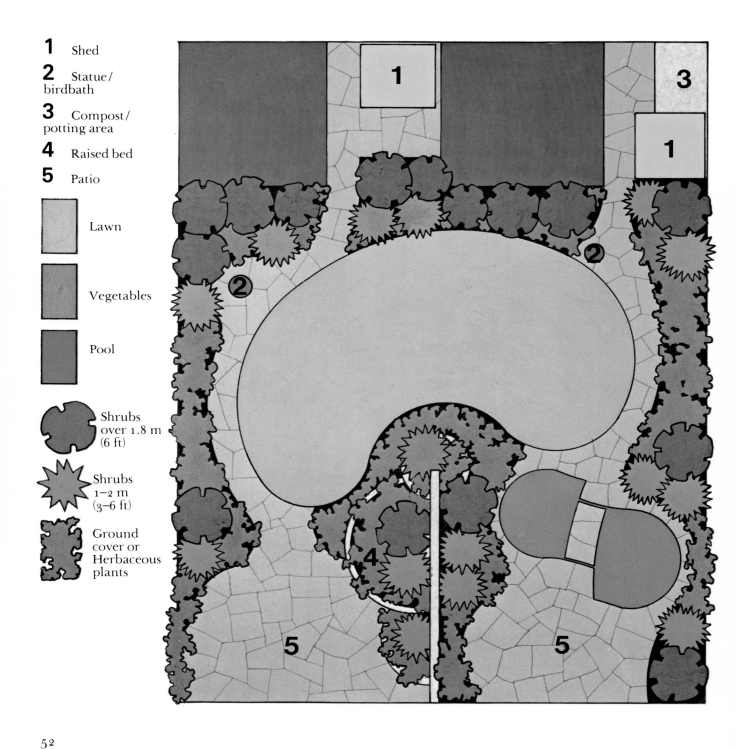

1 Shed

2 Statue/
birdbath

3 Compost/
potting area

4 Raised bed

5 Patio

Lawn

Vegetables

Pool

Shrubs
over 1.8 m
(6 ft)

Shrubs
1–2 m
(3–6 ft)

Ground
cover or
Herbaceous
plants

Climbers decorate the wall, whose expanse can additionally be relieved by two or more 'windows' with grilles.

This is the view from the patio of the left-hand garden, as one would gaze around the end of the dividing wall. Imagine how different the vista would be were the wall (or fence, or hedge) continued the whole length of the plot! But by using the artifice of 'twinning', the garden takes on an air of almost infinite space ... How far does the lawn extend? What lies beyond the tall shrubs away to the right? Where does the little gate at the end of the path lead to?

'Twinning' is not, admittedly, for the family with small chidren or pets that need to be confined. But there must be hundreds of thousands of homes that would be enriched by the linking of neighbouring gardens.

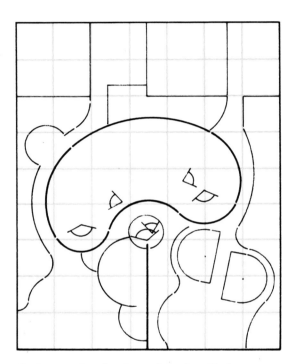

Setting-out plan showing radial points. Each square represents 2 × 2 m.

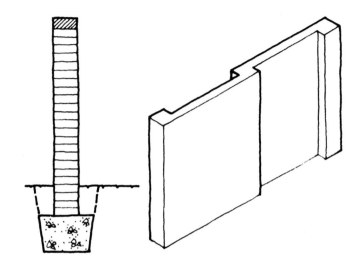

The wall shown is 150 cm (5 ft) high and 300 cm (10 ft) long. Dig a trench 60 cm (2 ft) deep and 45 cm (1 ft 6 in.) wide and half fill it with concrete (1 part cement, 2 parts sand, 4 parts coarse aggregate).

It is advisable to use a good brick that will stand up to frost and continual weathering. Lay with mortar consisting of 1 part cement, 1 part lime, 6 parts builder's sand. The wall, 11 cm (4½ in.) thick, should have 22 cm (9 in.) square piers at each end and in the middle. It is sometimes necessary, if a cheaper brick has been used, to finish the top of the wall with a course of engineering bricks as a coping.

Free-standing wall: Before building a boundary wall, check with the local authority and your house deeds for any height restriction. Also get approval from the local Technical Service Department – and your neighbour.

11 Small Town Garden

Because of the limited length of plots on new housing estates, gardens as broad as they are long (or almost so) are becoming increasingly common. The size is often no more than eight metres (25 feet) square, and this involves careful planning – not only in the design, but in the planting.

In the plan we show, spaces are created for various purposes, and maximum use of them is made. Curves defeat the square outline of the plot. Tiny lawns, especially in urban areas, are rarely successful, and gravel has been substituted. Spaces not used for permanent planting are paved with warm-coloured brick. This allows the introduction of a variety of containers, both for ornamental plants, and for the growing of fruit and vegetables (e.g., tomato tubs, strawberry and potato barrels). These can be arranged to suit both the aspect and the wishes of the owner.

A single tree – more would overcrowd the plot – provides a focal point and shade for the seat beneath it. A pool, complementary in shape to that of the gravel area, provides extra interest and, if a small fountain were incorporated, movement and sound.

Care must be taken not to plant shrubs that would, in time, tend to 'take over' and prove an embarrassment. At the same time, the more solid the planting at the rear of the garden (providing there is no view to be preserved) the better, since the boundary fence or wall can thus be hidden, and the impression given that more might lie beyond.

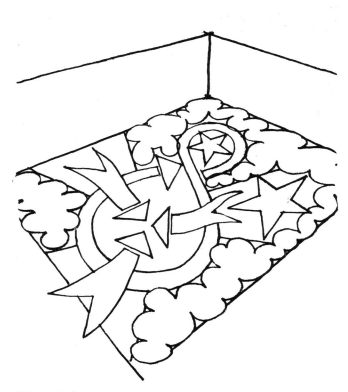

The main features of this small, squarish garden – the approach steps, the space for containers on the left, the ornamental pool, the shade seat – are set around the central meeting place, gravelled for all-weather use.

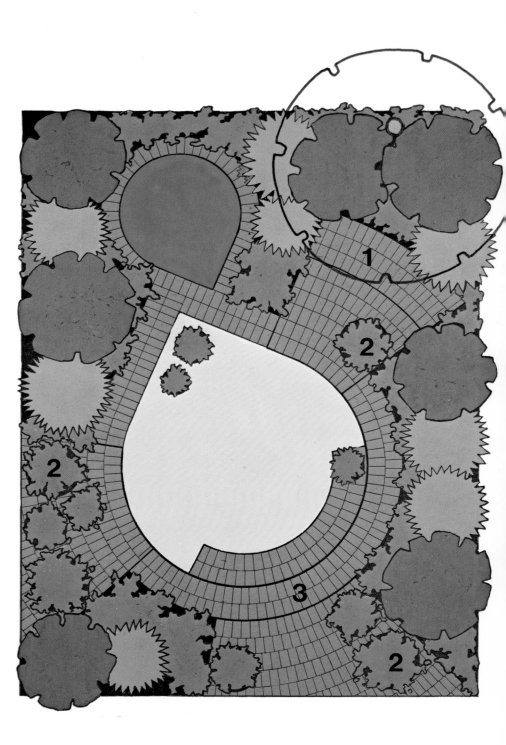

1 Brick bench
2 Tubs/pots
3 Steps

Brick

Gravel

Pool

Shrubs over 1.8 m (6 ft)

Shrubs 1–2 m (3–6 ft)

Ground cover or Herbaceous plants

This design was translated into fact at the 1980 Chelsea Show and won a top award. The use of warm-coloured brickwork and the sympathetic planting created the feeling of tranquil seclusion desirable in a town (or indeed, any) garden.

Although small, this is a garden that can provide a great deal of interest to the plant enthusiast, as well as a peaceful retreat from the noise and bustle of town life.

Containers with seasonal planting provide extra colour to complement the background of shrubs, chosen for their all-year-round interest. The pool is sited close to the seat so that all the activity that water attracts can be in view. Maintenance is at a very low level – a fact that the busy town-dweller will appreciate.

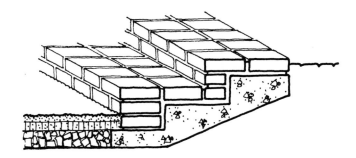

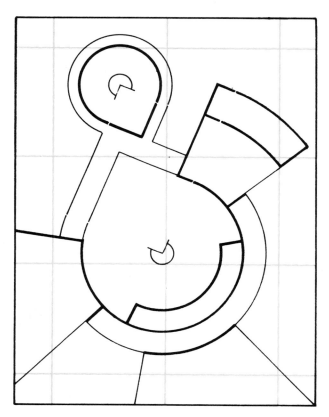

Setting-out plan showing radial points. Each square represents 2 × 2 m.

Brick steps: The 'tread' or 'going' of steps should be far deeper than those inside a building. They not only look better but are easier to walk up.

Form a concrete base with 32 cm (13 in.) treads and 15 cm (6 in.) risers. Bed the bricks (frost-resistant type) with mortar (1 part cement, 4 parts sand).

12 Garden for a Widening Plot

By no means all plots are of regular, rectangular shape. And that may not be a bad thing, especially if the plot widens out generously: for then the designer has the opportunity to use the extra space to create the illusion that the garden is much bigger than it really is. Study our design and imagine that you are looking at the view from the patio. The immediate prospect is a semi-circular lawn and a pool of the same shape – the lower half of the 'S' theme – with a rich, solid backing of conifers and shrubs behind the curving path. You might think this screen marks the rear boundary of the plot ... were it not for the glimpse of a further curving lawn with more trees beyond. And what is the significance of the pergola – is it guarding the entrance to an unseen part of the garden? How far does the lawn sweep round, what lies at the end of it? Is there, hidden away, a kitchen garden, a greenhouse?

All these questions compel you to set off to explore the garden – to satisfy your curiosity. And that means the design has succeeded in one of its major intentions. With the advantage of a plan view, you can see all the answers – that the pergola does indeed provide the threshold to the utility section, so well concealed; that the lawn does, of course, end in an intimate shrub-lined corner.

Although conifers, ornamental trees and shrubs must form the basis of the planting, the owner of this garden has plenty of scope for introducing roses or herbaceous plants, while that extra space in the widening plot will grow a lot of food.

A garden carefully balanced around an S shape which carries the eye through and beyond the starred focal points.

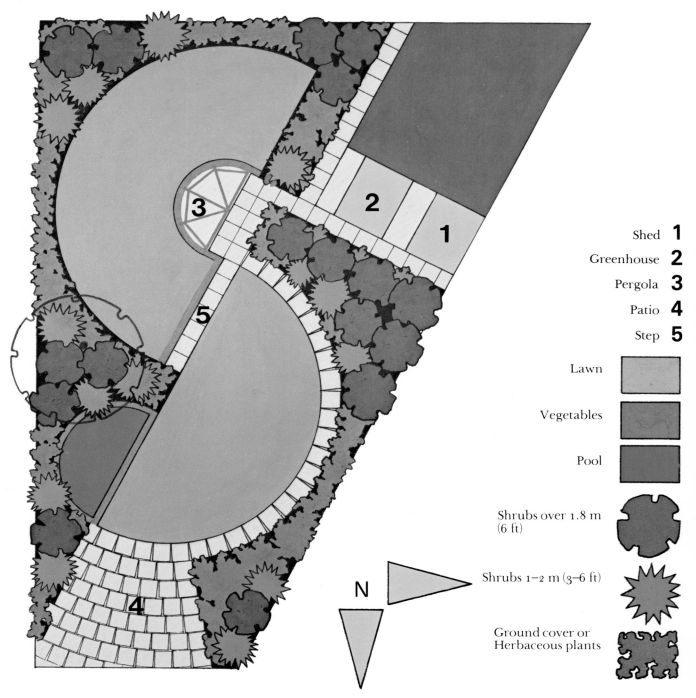

Shed **1**

Greenhouse **2**

Pergola **3**

Patio **4**

Step **5**

Lawn

Vegetables

Pool

Shrubs over 1.8 m
(6 ft)

Shrubs 1–2 m (3–6 ft)

N

Ground cover or
Herbaceous plants

12. GARDEN FOR A WIDENING PLOT

A picture that tells its own story – of a beautiful garden that asks to be explored. It offers the promise that the stroll will be fully rewarded.

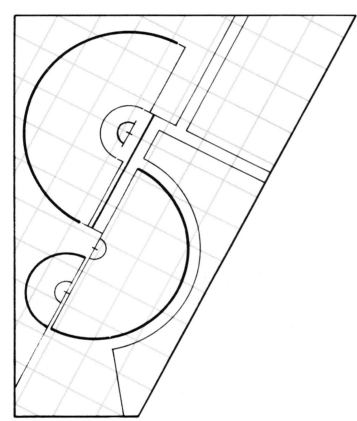

Setting-out plan showing radial points. Each square represents 2 × 2 m.

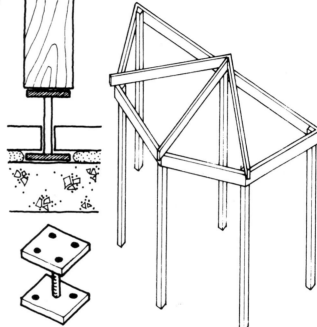

Pergola: Use planed softwood as follows:

Six 7.5 × 7.5 × 220 cm (3 in. × 3 in. × 7 ft) posts;
Four 15 × 2.5 × 120 cm (6 in. × 1 in. × 4 ft)
perimeter members;
One 15 × 2.5 × 300 cm (6 in. × 1 in. × 10 ft)
member;
Three 15 × 2.5 × 150 cm (6 in. × 1 in. × 5 ft)
members.

To prevent rotting of timber posts at ground level, mild steel 'shoes' can be screwed to the bottom of the posts and bolted into the concrete base: or use Metposts, steel sockets let into the ground.

13 Garden for a Narrowing Plot

The positioning of the summer house is no accident. It provides a pleasing prospect – the pool with its central fountain or statue, the lawns, the shrubs or roses on the far side – and the eye is taken away from the narrower area. The plot that seemed so unpromising has yielded a garden full of promise!

The plot that narrows is by no means uncommon – you'll find one or more on every housing estate. And the owner usually wishes he hadn't got it, fearing the difficulty of making an attractive garden within its limiting boundaries. Our design shows one way in which the problems can be solved. First note that, contrary to what you might expect, a geometrical theme has been chosen for the geometrical type of plot. This concentrates the eye on the shapes within the garden rather than on the triangular nature of its boundaries. So we have lawns of octagonal shape, attended by an octagonal pool – the whole served by square paving stones. Next observe that, from the house windows or the patio, the eye is drawn to the summer house and the long border that embraces it rather than to the narrow part of the garden. But it is by no means obvious that the plot is all that narrow at the end – or that it ends at all at the convergance of the two boundaries. The path disappearing between the closely planted trees and shrubs is designed to deceive the eye into recognising that much more might lie beyond. In fact there are only the vegetable plot and the compost heap – important though they are.

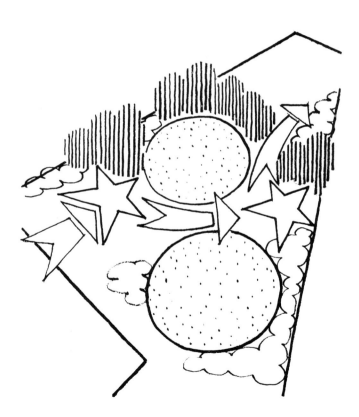

The arrows clearly show how the eye will move through this garden whilst registering the starred focal points.

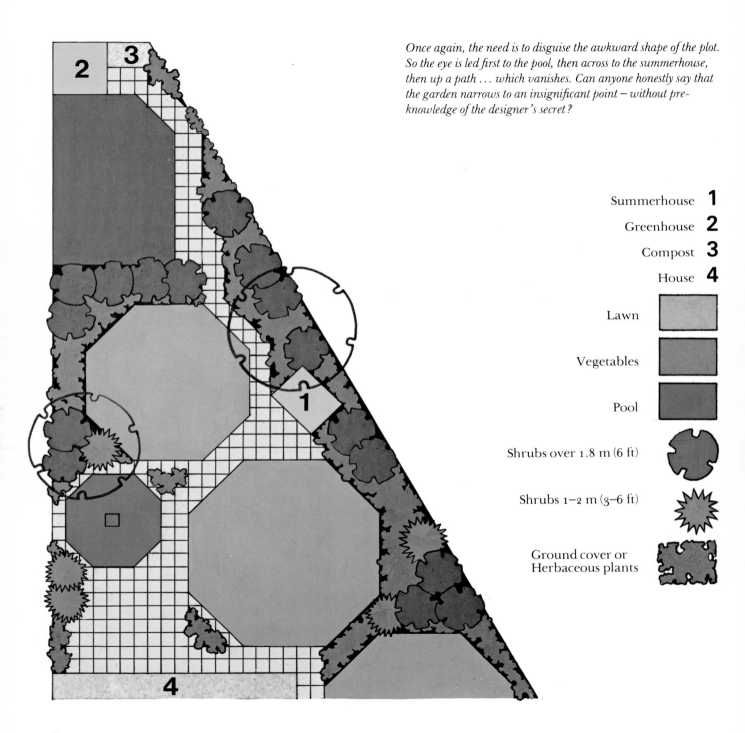

Once again, the need is to disguise the awkward shape of the plot. So the eye is led first to the pool, then across to the summerhouse, then up a path ... which vanishes. Can anyone honestly say that the garden narrows to an insignificant point — without pre-knowledge of the designer's secret ?

Summerhouse **1**

Greenhouse **2**

Compost **3**

House **4**

Lawn

Vegetables

Pool

Shrubs over 1.8 m (6 ft)

Shrubs 1–2 m (3–6 ft)

Ground cover or
Herbaceous plants

The drawing of the garden as seen from the
house windows emphasises the importance of the
summerhouse in the design. The angle at which it
is approached by the path dividing the twin lawns
distracts the mind from any thoughts of the
garden's increasing narrowness.

This apart, the summerhouse offers a very
pleasant reverse view across the wider part of the
garden.

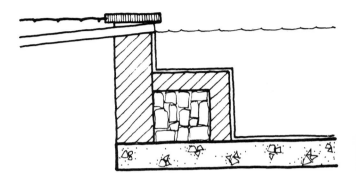

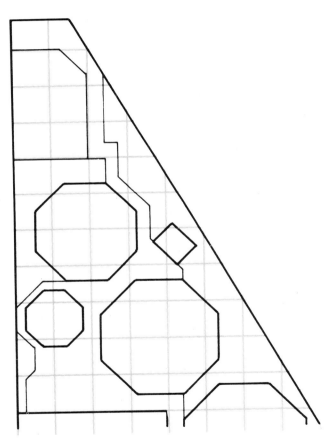

Setting-out plan. Each square represents 2 × 2 m.

Formal pool: Procedure if a concrete pool is preferred to one using a flexible liner:

Form a 15 cm (6 in.) thick concrete base (1:2:4 cement: sand: aggregate). Lay 20 cm (8 in.) dense concrete block or brick sides with hardcore infill.

Overflow: 5 cm (2 in.) diameter PVC pipe is set at the required water level and takes excess water underground to a soakaway (a deep hole filled with hardcore).

Line the interior of the pool with a sand/cement render mixed with a proprietary waterproofing agent.

14 Garden for a Young Couple

Marriage brings its problems – not least of which is the planning and laying out of the plot on which the new home is built. It's all the more difficult because, in almost every case, neither partner has had any experience of gardening and plants, let alone design. So, if they are to be helped, it must be with a simple plan and straightforward planting, offering easy upkeep. But they will also want an attractive garden, with a spacious leisure area where they can relax, have summer meals and entertain their friends.

The design we show meets all these needs – in a plot that can be as small as 12 by 8 metres (40 by 27 feet), a not uncommon size these days. The patio is cleanly paved, with an L-shaped pool to cool it and give interest. (If preferred, this could be omitted and replaced with tubs or other containers for seasonal flowers.) Screening the area, on the left, is a fence with climbers, while a wall of openwork blocks, pierced by an arch that gives an intriguing glimpse of the garden beyond. This is approached by stepping stones across the pool. The open side gives on to a level lawn which sweeps round behind the screen wall, inviting inspection of the hidden part of the garden.

The planting is simple, requiring little upkeep and relying, in the main, on two ornamental trees, shrubs, and – along the border on the right – roses. Ground cover is used where possible although, with so little maintenance needed, the newly-weds may well be willing to tackle any weeding as a form of gentle relaxation.

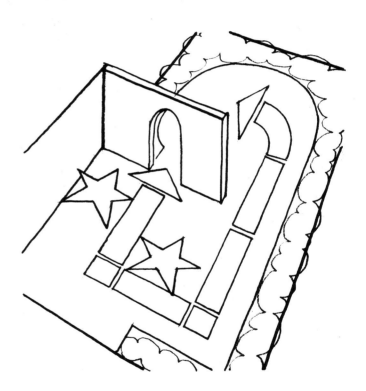

The wall may seem something of a luxury, but it serves many purposes. It cosily contains the paved area, where meals can be taken and friends entertained; the archway offers inviting glimpses of the garden beyond; and the wall can host attractive climbing plants.

1 Seat

2 Arch in wall

3 Climbers

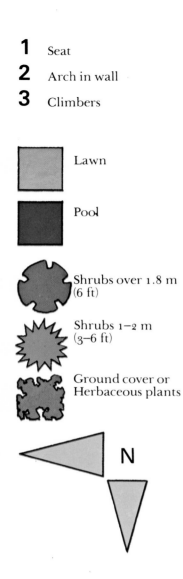

Lawn

Pool

Shrubs over 1.8 m (6 ft)

Shrubs 1–2 m (3–6 ft)

Ground cover or Herbaceous plants

N

The plan shows that this is a garden simple to lay out and straightforward to plant. The young couple will enjoy the limited amount of work necessary and find a speedy reward for their labours.

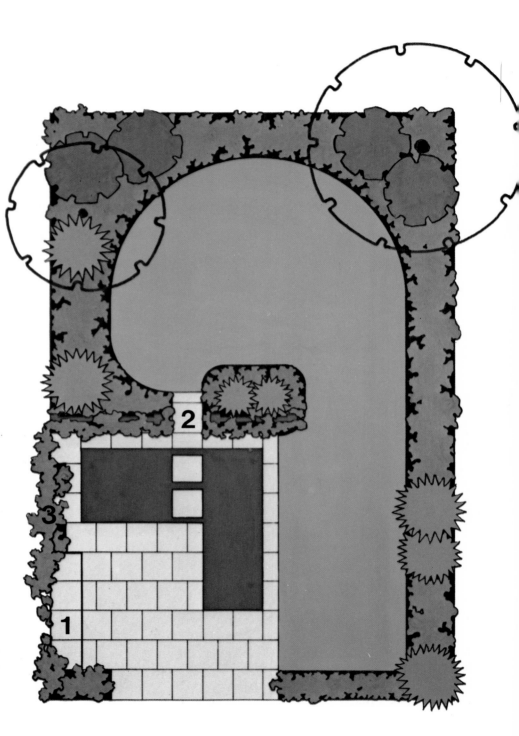

Most young couples have to start off with a small house. And there's no better way of increasing the available space than by creating an outdoor living room. That is exactly what this design succeeds in doing. Sunshine is trapped, cold winds are warded off, paving allows use after rain, pools and grass bring coolness in hot weather. Here is a place where life can be lived in comfort for many weeks of the year and where informal parties can be held – in much the same way as the Romans passed their leisure hours in their open courtyards.

So there it is – an easily run garden, a pleasing garden, a garden in which the young couple will soon take pride.

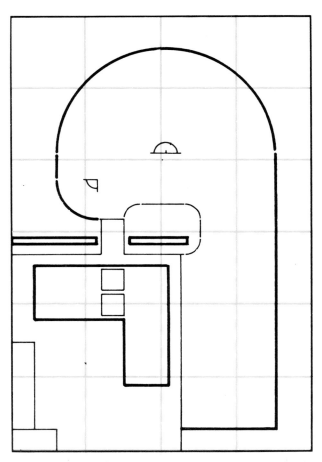

Setting-out plan showing radial points. Each square represents 2 × 2 m.

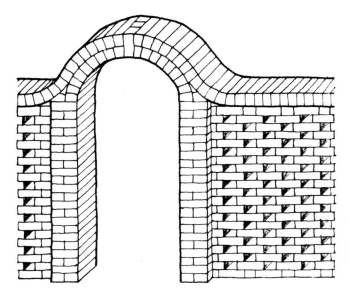

Brick screen and archway: Build brick piers to each side of the archway and at each end of the screen, 23 × 23 cm (9 × 9 in.) building up the walling with 11.5 cm (4½ in.) 'honeycomb' brickwork.

Build the arch with two courses of 23 cm (9 in.) bricks. A temporary timber semi-circular frame should be used to support the brickwork while it sets, and ensure that a true arch is constructed. Notice the 'key' brick in the centre of the arch.

15 Garden for a Growing Family

Keen gardeners with a young family have problems to face over a number of years – problems that are ever changing. The garden must provide facilities for play from an early age – and different kinds of play. At the same time the parents, if they value their garden, will not want to sacrifice all its beauty and the pleasure they derive from gardening – a situation that happens all too often, partly because of inadequate design. The larger the garden, the easier it becomes to cater for children. It is the small garden that presents the difficulties.

The design we show tackles them in two ways: the provision of areas for play, and planting that is not too vulnerable – both of which are capable of being easily changed – all within the framework of an attractive lay-out. Two very shallow steps (rounded with no sharp corners) lead on to a smooth paved terrace in an arm of which is sited a sandpit, simply converted into a paddling pool later, and finally into an ornamental one. The lawn, at first, is a plain, kidney-shaped one on which games can be played. Later, it is suggested that a shrub peninsula be built out into it, to give better concealment of the greenhouse and shed, and to give an air of mystery. Beyond the lawn and to the right is a Wendy house (always a favourite with children), which can be replaced by a summerhouse later. The rear area has many possibilities. Until the toddler stage is passed, the whole might well be devoted to food-growing. Later it could become a play area, perhaps with a swing or slide, or even a brick wall – always popular – against which a ball can be bounced or small cricket played (don't forget to protect the greenhouse!). Or again, the space might be shared between play and vegetables. When, finally, the children grow up, the whole area becomes available for food.

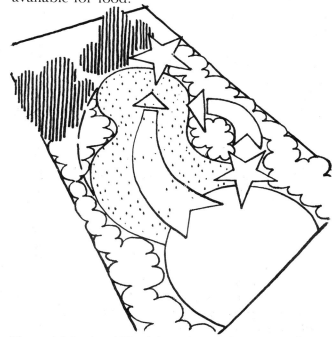

The sandpit/pool and Wendy house/summerhouse are the focal features.

1 Summerhouse

2 Greenhouse

3 Shed

4 Refuse

5 Compost

6 Patio

7 Steps

8 Play area

 Lawn

 Vegetables

 Pool

 Shrubs over 1.8 m (6 ft)

 Shrubs 1–2 m (3–6 ft)

 Ground cover or Herbaceous border

A garden for the family should appeal to and interest all its members – from the youngest to the oldest. Here there is space and opportunity for children's games and amusement, room for Mother to relax (while keeping an eye on the toddlers), and space for Father to grow flowers and vegetables.

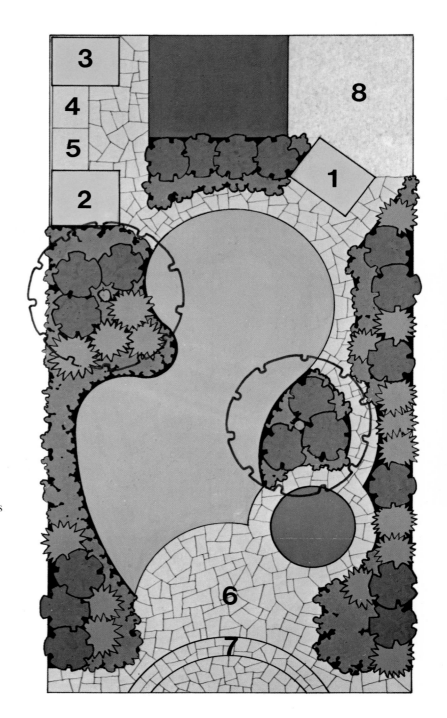

For some years, the planting emphasis should be on small trees and shrubs, with only thornless roses and low-growing perennials. As the children learn to respect plants, choicer subjects can increasingly be used.

All families grow up – and so do gardens. By the time the trees and shrubs have matured, the children will have lost interest in either sandpit or paddling pool, and the Wendy house. So an ornamental pool and a summerhouse can take their places in a well-established garden of real attraction.

It may be that the lawn – used so long for hectic ball games – will need reseeding with a fine-grass mixture. And the opportunity can be taken to introduce less robust but desirable plants which in earlier years had little chance of survival.

In the end, it becomes a pleasant and enjoyable garden for retirement – with only the grandchildren to worry about …

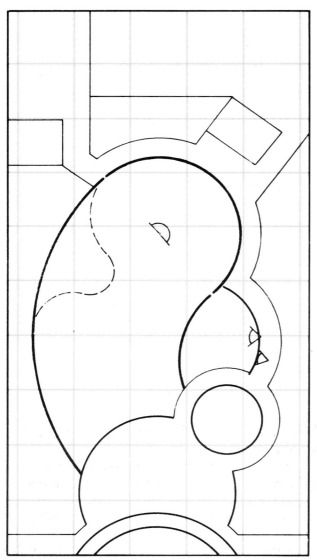

Setting-out plan showing radial points. Each square represents 2 × 2 m.

Sandpit/Pool: A well-drained sandpit surrounded by paving is easily constructed, and can readily be adapted to make a formal pool in later years.

Excavate a circle 70 cm (2 ft 4 in.) deep. Place concrete 15 cm (6 in.) deep and 40 cm (16 in.) wide around the edge to form the foundation for the low wall. Lay clean rubble or broken bricks in the bottom of the excavation to the level of the foundation.

Using 20 cm (8 in.) thick concrete blocks or bricks, build up the retaining walls to 7 cm (3 in.) below ground level. Place 4 cm (1½ in.) precast paving slabs in the bottom leaving 1 cm (½ in.) gaps for good drainage. Bed the surrounding paving on mortar. Fill the pit with clean coarse sand as desired.

To convert to a pool, lift the surrounding paving, spread 5 cm (2 in.) of sand over the floor and lay a butyl liner, re-laying the paving stones to overlap the edge.

16 Formal Garden

Amenities include, on one side of the patio, a small pool and on the other, a permanent barbecue. Instead of a vegetable plot, an area is provided – alongside the bench – for containers in which tomatoes, potatoes and other crops can be grown.

One has only to travel by train through any suburban district to notice how dull and unimaginative are the rows of back gardens. Nearly all are, of course, rectangular plots – some short, some long – but in almost every case the lawn follows the lines of the fence on each side, and is bounded by narrow, straight borders. It's almost as if the owners are hypnotised by the strict rectangularity of their piece of land. But why not, if formality appeals, base the design on other geometrical shapes – the circle, for instance, as in our suggested plan? Here two circular lawns are linked in simple but intriguing fashion by a path that leads from the brick-paved patio around one side of the first lawn and then divides to encompass an architectural feature (statue, sundial or bird bath) before resuming its passage around the further lawn, and thence to the sheltered, three-sided bench – a pleasant spot in which to rest and gaze back down the garden. The twin circles within the rectangular plot create interesting shapes for the planting of trees – one on each side – shrubs, roses and herbaceous subjects. The central feature simply begs to be surrounded with massed geraniums or petunias in summer and daffodils, hyacinths or tulips in spring.

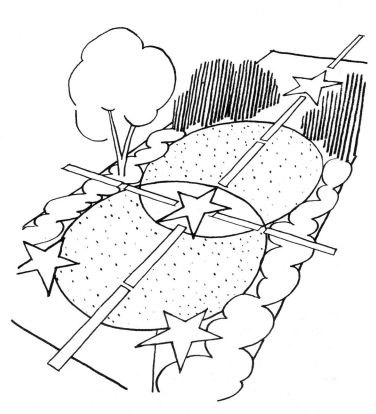

Formality appeals to many gardeners, and the main features in this garden are carefully disposed around and on the central axis, culminating in the three-sided, sheltered bench at the far end.

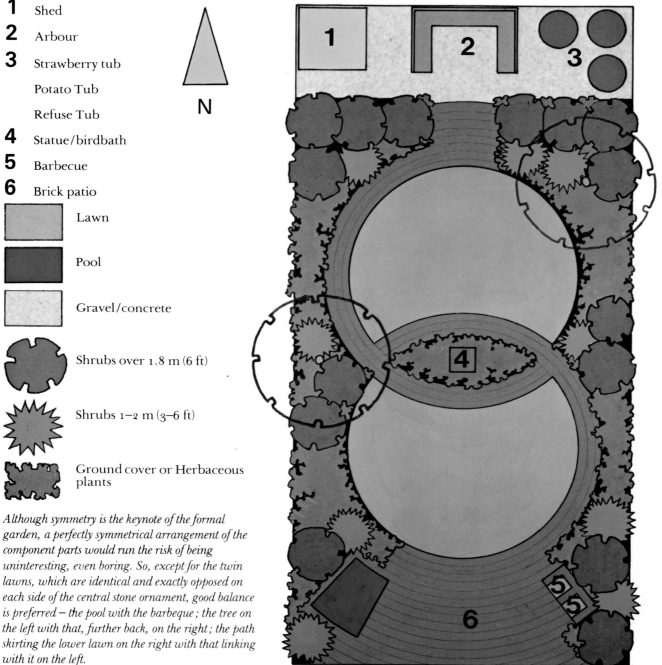

1 Shed
2 Arbour
3 Strawberry tub
  Potato Tub
  Refuse Tub
4 Statue/birdbath
5 Barbecue
6 Brick patio

N

Lawn

Pool

Gravel/concrete

Shrubs over 1.8 m (6 ft)

Shrubs 1–2 m (3–6 ft)

Ground cover or Herbaceous plants

Although symmetry is the keynote of the formal garden, a perfectly symmetrical arrangement of the component parts would run the risk of being uninteresting, even boring. So, except for the twin lawns, which are identical and exactly opposed on each side of the central stone ornament, good balance is preferred – the pool with the barbecue; the tree on the left with that, further back, on the right; the path skirting the lower lawn on the right with that linking with it on the left.

Seen from the house or patio, the effect is that of a green-carpeted stage, with colourful, graceful scenery and interesting props – the quiet pool on the left, the brick barbecue opposite, the central statue, sundial or bird bath, the seat dominating the backcloth. It is not difficult to imagine the players – family, friends – who will bring the stage to life with pleasant informality.

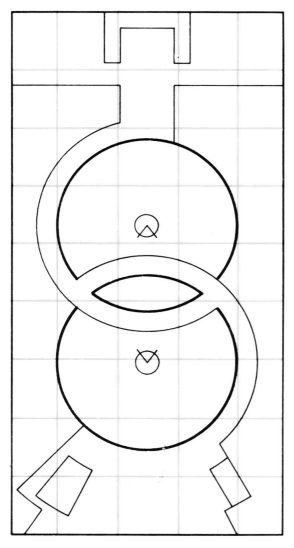

Setting-out plan showing radial points. Each square represents 2 × 2 m.

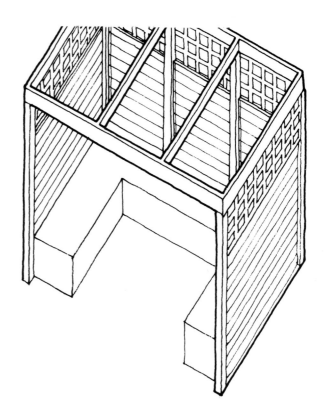

Arbour: Overall dimensions: 300 cm (10 ft) long, 198 cm (6 ft 6 in.) deep, 260 cm (8 ft 6 in.) high.

Materials: Two panels of standard fencing 183 × 183 cm (6 × 6 ft); three 183 × 60 cm (6 × 2 ft) standard trellis panels; three 90 × 60 cm (3 × 2 ft) trellis panels; six 7.5 × 7.5 × 245 cm (3 in. × 3 in. × 8 ft) high posts; four 15 × 2.5 × 198 cm (6 in. × 1 in. × 6 ft 6 in.) lengths of planed soft wood to form the top of the frame.

17 Garden for a Retired Couple

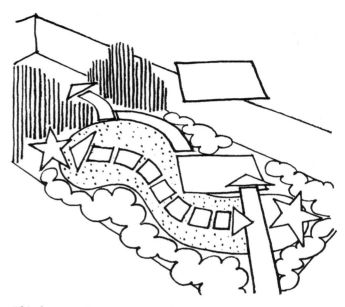

This design, suited to a narrow plot, attracts the eye along the arrows to the starred focal points. It would fit the plots on which so many semi-detached houses are built. The limitations of the plot are disguised by the disposition of the spaces, the starred features, the outlines and the angles at which they are set.

There comes a time when, however willing the spirit, the flesh is not up to putting in the number of hours in the garden it did. In other words, it is a time when leisure is all-important. So the need for the retired (or ageing) couple is a garden that is tranquil, restful and easily run.

A major part of the design with these aims in mind is taken up with a stone-and-brick patio (pergola-covered to provide shelter, dappled shade, and space for entertaining), a semi-circular pool, and a long, curving lawn – all capable of easy maintenance. The same can be said of the planting – trees, shrubs, some perennials, all thickly mulched to deter weeds.

Even retired people enjoy growing a few vegetables, and pottering in a greenhouse. Provision is made for both – though, with digging in mind, the area of the kitchen garden is kept small, but still large enough to give supplies of vegetables and fruit for many months of the year. And that is important for people old enough and with time enough, to appreciate the freshness and flavour of home-grown food.

Yet the accent, in this garden, is on freedom: freedom to do only as much or little work as the happy couple feel like, freedom – and space – to laze, to sleep, to dream.

1 Greenhouse

2 Patio with pergola

3 Seat or Statue

 Lawn

 Vegetables

 Pool

 Gravel/concrete

 Shrubs over 1.8 m (6 ft)

 Shrubs 1–2 m (3–6 ft)

 Ground cover or Herbaceous plants

 N

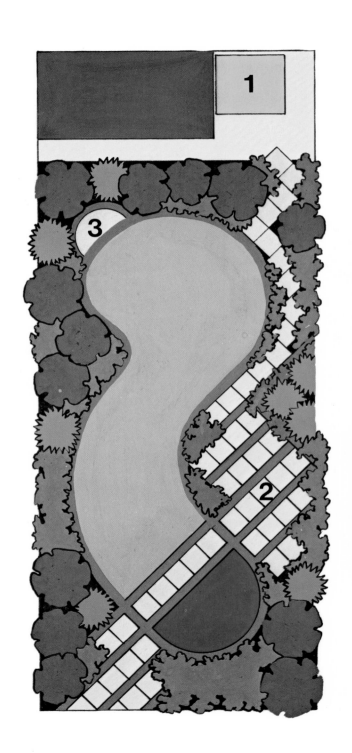

The patio is the central feature of this design, the climber-clad pergola offering the quiet, sheltered retreat which a retired couple can enjoy to the full. It commands a view of the garden in all directions, from the pool to the focal point of the statue or birdbath. All is linked by the curving lawn. Bold, close planting hides and protects the productive plot and the greenhouse or shed.

Our retired couple, relaxing on the patio, command a view of the garden in all directions. All is linked by the curving lawn. Bold, close planting hides and protects the productive plot and the greenhouse or shed.

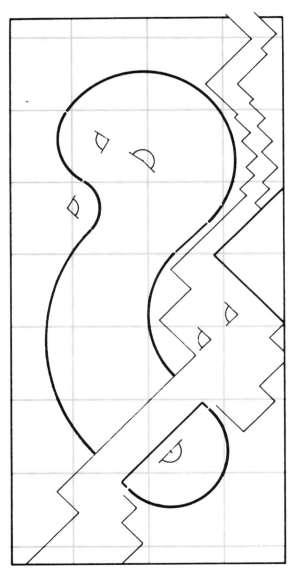

Setting-out plan showing radial points. Each square represents 2 × 2 m.

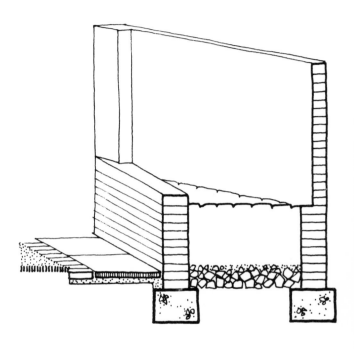

Raised planter/boundary wall: The construction is similar to that in Garden No. 10 except that the walling containing the soil should be 22 cm (9 in.) thick.

Before placing topsoil in the planter, fill the bottom with 10 cm (4 in.) of stones or rubble, covered with a layer of gravel and then sand. This will assist drainage, which will be further helped if a few vertical joints are left open just above ground level.

18 Low Maintenance Garden

One way to create a garden needing little maintenance is to let Nature take a prominent part. And that is the way chosen for our design for a plot of modest size. It is dominated by a mature tree (if this does not figure in your site, it is worth knowing that trees up to 6 metres (20 feet) tall can be ordered from, and planted by, specialist firms). Grass is, of course, the most natural cover for the major area of the garden – but grass needs frequent mowing. Choose it if you don't mind this quite pleasant exercise – an air cushion (hover) machine would be the most suitable kind. But gravel, which we have shown, needs no attention except an occasional raking and treatment once a year with a simazine weedkiller to keep it clean. Circular log cuts make an unusual and attractive pathway: unlike paving stones they need little or no sweeping, and preserve the natural appearance of the garden.

The bole of the tree is surrounded by a timber seat. Immediately behind is a raised bed of shrubs, retained by logs driven upright into the ground. Opposing the tree is a group of foliage shrubs, with climbers – which can be wisteria or clematis, firethorn or variegated ivy – although purists, wishing to conform with the natural theme, may prefer such hedgerow climbers as honeysuckle and sweet briar. The garden is approached by three gently angled steps, retained with stout logs and attended by groups of wooden tubs for shrubs, bulbs, crops, or seasonal flowers. The rear areas are occupied by a summerhouse (or shed) and, protected by a screen of bamboo, a space for compost heap or bonfire.

Whether in town, suburb or country, this garden can satisfy the yearning so often felt for a truly tranquil retreat from the bustle of life in the 80s.

This is not only the most natural-looking garden in our collection but the simplest design. Descend the broad steps and stroll down past the tree – the only major feature – till you come to the summerhouse. But, as you will see, there's more to it than that . . .

1 Summerhouse

2 Refuse and Potting

3 Bench under tree

4 Steps

5 Raised planter

 Gravel

 Logs

 Shrubs over 1.8 m (6 ft)

 Shrubs 1–2 m (3–6 ft)

 Ground cover or Herbaceous plants

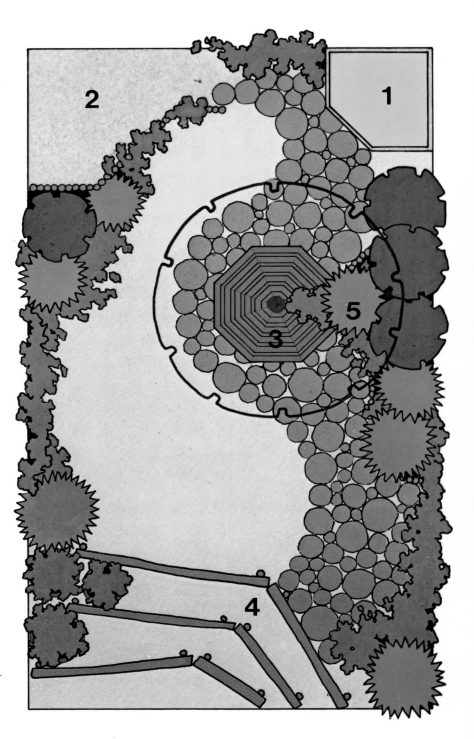

The plan shows the interesting use made of tree trunk off-cuts – a timber yard is the best source – which, carefully laid, provide an all-weather walk-way to the seating around the tree and the summerhouse beyond.

The Low Maintenance Garden could perhaps be called the Organised Wild Garden – for there's little doubt it will appeal to the lover of countryside plants, birds, and wildlife generally. It could, if you like, be planted entirely with species that are to be found growing in the woods, fields and hedgerows – though many would say it is a pity to deny ourselves the delights the hybridists have lavished upon us, just for the sake of a principle.

On the other hand, what a joy it is to be able to embrace the joys of the country within one's home boundaries!

In this context, we must remind you that it is illegal to dig up and remove any wild plant without the permission of the owner of the land. Fortunately many of the more common kinds are easily raised from seed, which one or two seed firms can supply.

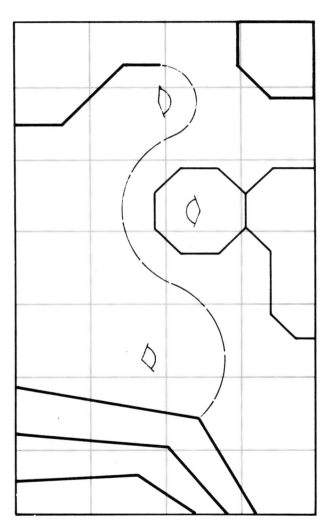

Setting-out plan showing radial points. Each square represents 2 × 2 m.

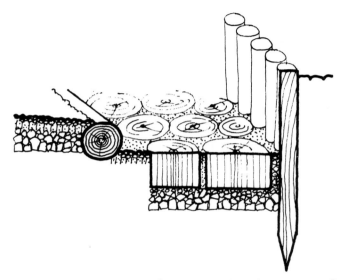

Log paving: Cut, or order, 15 cm (6 in.) sections of suitable tree trunks. Excavate 22 cm (9 in.) of soil. Lay 7 cm (3 in.) of crushed stone or gravel over the area to be paved to ensure good drainage. Lay the sections as close as possible and infill the gaps with gravel or stone chippings.

Log step: Set 15 cm (6 in.) diameter logs in place. Hammer in 5 × 5 × 30 cm (2 × 2 × 12 in.) stakes behind the ends of the logs and secure with strong nails. Backfill behind each log to form a step with 10 cm (4 in.) of hardcore, 2.5 cm (1 in.) of hoggin and 2.5 cm (1 in.) of gravel.

Raised bed: Hammer a row of 90 cm (36 in.) long and 50–70 cm (2–3 in.) diameter larch poles into the ground, and saw off level 45 cm (18 in.) above ground level. Infill with soil.

19 Garden for the Handicapped

The word 'handicapped' is often accepted as referring to someone in a wheelchair. And unfortunately this is sometimes true. But the word also embraces those afflicted by such disabling diseases as rheumatism and arthritis, and elderly people who may be healthy enough but can no longer bend, push a mower, or handle a spade. So our garden for the disabled is based on the conception of raised beds and borders, which can be tended without the need to stoop – if need be, from a wheelchair. Such beds have other advantages; they lend themselves to the creation of a garden of uncommon quality, in which plants thrive and flowers are closer to the eye and the nose.

A winding path, paved with tarmacadam or concrete and wide enough to be negotiated without difficulty, and with gentle ramps rather than steps, gives access to every part of the garden. Why have a sunken area necessitating these ramps? There's a practical answer: to provide enough soil to build up the raised beds, which are retained with brick or concrete blocks. Vegetables are grown on an island site and along a narrow border – both raised – so that all plants are easily reached, and picking or cutting is made simple. This area is screened from house and patio by the central 'peninsula' pushing out from beneath the branches of the tree, and the lesser promontory which edges out from the greenhouse (this has a door wide enough to admit a wheelchair).

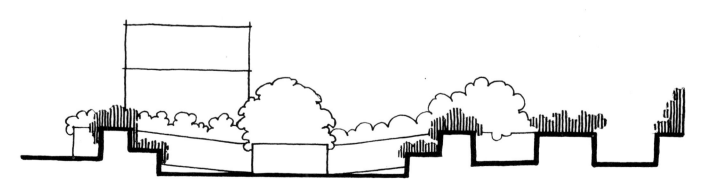

This section drawing shows how the beds are raised using soil excavated from the lower areas. But there are no steps, only gently-sloping ramps easily negotiated by wheelchairs, and making walking safer for the elderly and infirm.

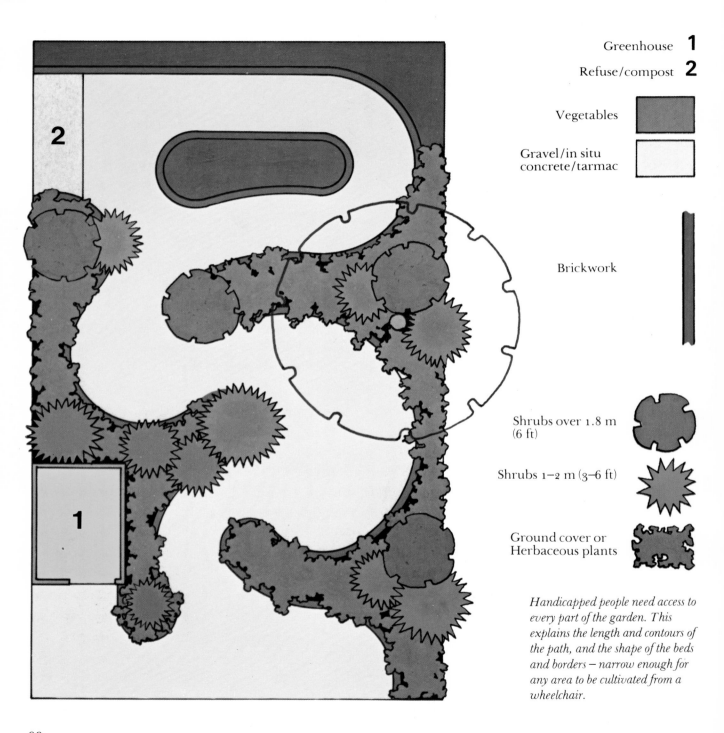

Greenhouse **1**

Refuse/compost **2**

Vegetables

Gravel/in situ
concrete/tarmac

Brickwork

Shrubs over 1.8 m
(6 ft)

Shrubs 1–2 m (3–6 ft)

Ground cover or
Herbaceous plants

*Handicapped people need access to
every part of the garden. This
explains the length and contours of
the path, and the shape of the beds
and borders – narrow enough for
any area to be cultivated from a
wheelchair.*

A garden for the handicapped is not going to look like a normal garden. But that does not mean it cannot be attractive and full of interest. The raised beds and borders can not only support almost every kind of tree and shrub, but often grow them better because of excellent drainage, improved light, and a free circulation of air. There is also the opportunity to use plants which can tumble seductively over the retaining walls.

A greenhouse is a place in which a handicapped person can spend many happy hours. A door wide enough for the wheelchair is, of course, essential. So are a wide interior path and low benches – necessities which may well require a custom built house, or modifications to a standard model.

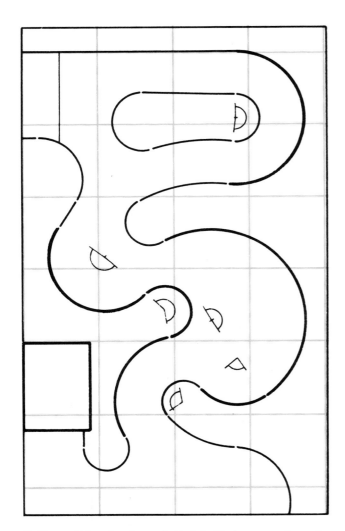

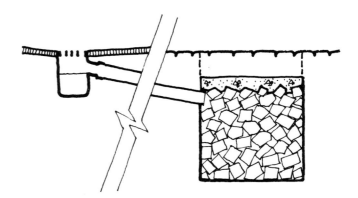

Gulley and soakaway: Dig a hole $75 \times 75 \times 90$ cm ($30 \times 30 \times 36$ in.) deep and fill it with stones or rubble to within 20 cm (8 in.) of ground level. Place 5 cm (2 in.) of concrete over this and fill up with topsoil. Set the yard gulley at the lowest point and connect to the soakaway with 10 cm (4 in.) diameter PVC pipe, laid to a fall of 2.5 cm in 150 cm (one inch in 5 feet).

Setting-out plan showing radial points. Each square represents 2×2 m.

20 The Productive Garden

While a garden capable of supplying the family with all the vegetables and fruit it needs is rarely an actual necessity, it obviously has its attractions. Indeed, it is not uncommon to find a gardener who confesses that growing food, rather than flowers, is his main interest. But that gardener is rarely a woman, and so – between husband and wife – a compromise is desirable.

The garden we show is based on one designed for the Daily Express, and which won a gold medal at the 1977 Chelsea Show. In this modified version, a lawn replaces part of what was a very spacious paved patio, and there is a larger area for vegetables. At the same time, the garden is visually attractive.

The off-set axis not only draws attention from the rectangular lines of the plot but introduces some interesting shapes which are put to good use. The patio, with barbeque, is sheltered by a vine-covered pergola. This is extended around the lawn, to the path which leads off from it, and links with a line of posts bordering the major vegetable plot (screened by cordon fruit) and the soft fruit plot (protected by a netted cage). Across the lawn are the greenhouse, cold frame and herb garden – all conveniently near the house. Behind the main lawn is a smaller area which can be used either as a second lawn (useful for a swing, slide or climbing frame if there are young children), a second vegetable plot, or small orchard (using trees on dwarfing root stocks).

The ornamental planting is provided by a border of shrubs and herbaceous plants reaching from the patio, which it partially screens, to the fruit plot and to climbing roses or other climbers on the posts.

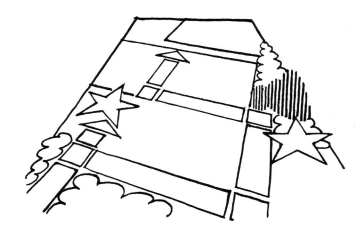

The two key 'landmarks' are the pergola-covered patio on the right (leisure) and the greenhouse/frame area on the left (productivity).

1 Shed

2 Compost

3 Greenhouse

4 Cold frame

5 Barbecue

6 Pergola

 Lawn

 Vegetables

 Fruit cage

 Shrubs over 1.8 m (6 ft)

 Shrubs 1–2 m (3–6 ft)

 Ground cover or Herbaceous plants

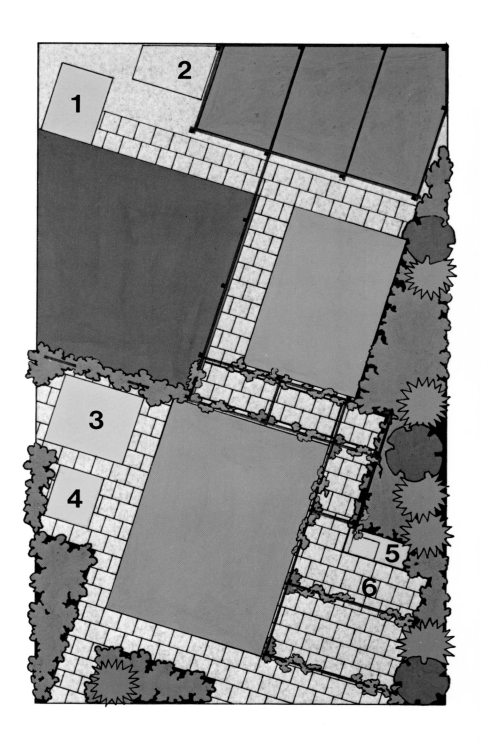

The keen grow-your-own-food gardener may well want to use the space allotted to a second lawn for further vegetables. It is easily converted back to grass, or into a mini-orchard, when the family gets smaller – or energy decreases.

The view from the house gives no hint of the amount of space devoted to food production. This is effected by the introduction of the pergola, with its clothing of vines (themselves productive) and climbing roses; the continuation of the posts leading from it in two directions; and the screen of shrubs on the right and the cordon fruit on the left.

A feature of the garden is the dry access to all parts afforded by the paving. If the initial expense of this is considered too high, the service paths to the greenhouse and the productive areas could be gravelled, and perhaps converted later.

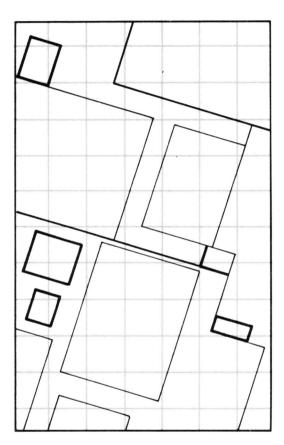

Setting-out plan. Each square represents 2 × 2 m.

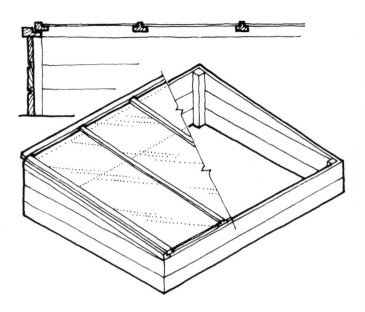

Nail 15 × 2.5 cm (6 × 1 in.) shiplap boarding (available from a timber merchant) to 5 × 5 cm (2 × 2 in.) corner members. Fix 7.5 × 5 cm (3 × 2 in.) rebated runners to each side.

Buy ready-made rebated lengths to form a frame for the glazing as follows: One 150 cm (5 ft) and two 120 cm (4 ft) lengths of 5 × 2.5 cm (2 × 1 in.) single rebate sections for the perimeter; two 120 cm (4 ft) lengths of 5 × 2.5 cm (2 × 1 in.) double rebate sections for intermediate members; one 150 cm (5 ft) length of 5 × 1.8 cm (2 × ¼ in.) front edge.

Fix 'greenhouse' grade glass with sprigs and putty-in.

Cold frame: Overall size: 150 × 120 cm (5 × 4 ft); 45 cm (18in.) at the back and 30 cm (1 ft) at the front.

21 Garden with the Accent on Water

There's a magic about water that cannot be denied. It offers reflections, movement, music – and tranquillity. So it is not surprising that, to many, it is a highly desirable feature of the modern garden. The garden we show will be recognised by visitors to the 1979 Chelsea Flower Show as the one designed for the Daily Express by Guy Farthing, and which won for them a gold medal for the third year running.

There are three linked pools, all hexagonal in shape and conforming with the geometrical theme on which the design is based. The upper, right-hand, pool has a bubbling fountain which sends the water cascading into the middle pool and thence – stilled by the stepping stone bridge – to the third pool from which it is invisibly pumped back to the first pool.

Inevitably there is a great deal of paving, for it is no good having a sophisticated arrangement of pools without plenty of space surrounding it – space for relaxing and listening to the splashing of the water, for eating meals in its presence, for watching the darting movement of fish, dragon flies and other wildlife that water always attracts.

Yet the water feature is but a component part – though an important one – of a garden whose twin lawns, trees, shrubs and roses, flower-filled

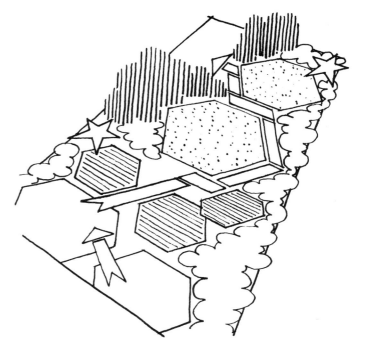

The arrows show the eye's movement and the stars, the two focal points.

containers and productive area combine to create a garden that is both beautiful and exciting.

There are two focal points in this garden. If you sit on the elevated right-hand part of the patio, your gaze will be focused on the sheltered seat overlooking the left-hand pool. But take the two steps down to the lower area and you find yourself looking over the stepping-stone bridge and across the twin lawns to the statuary in the distant right-hand corner.

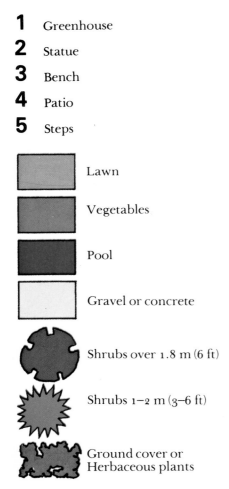

1 Greenhouse

2 Statue

3 Bench

4 Patio

5 Steps

Lawn

Vegetables

Pool

Gravel or concrete

Shrubs over 1.8 m (6 ft)

Shrubs 1–2 m (3–6 ft)

Ground cover or
Herbaceous plants

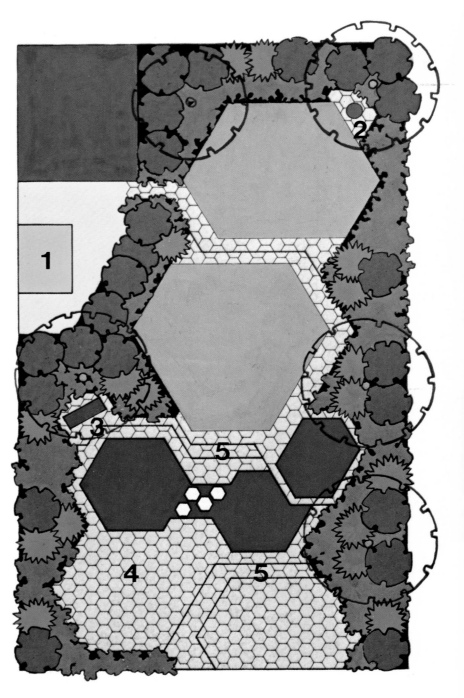

*The plan view reveals how the garden is
based on the concept of the hexagon. But it is
not so geometrically exact that the hexagons are
all perfect shapes: the fact cannot be detected
at eye level and is in any case unnecessary.*

It is conceded that this is not a cheap garden to lay out, mainly because of the large number of paving stones needed. But, as was proved at the Chelsea Show, it has great character and charm, and the years of enjoyment it will provide may be thought to justify the initial cost.

The spacious, split-level patio offers full scope for outdoor leisure pursuits, and the entertainment of friends in gracious style. Not every garden can provide the music of water in such a setting as accompaniment to a summer's evening barbecue!

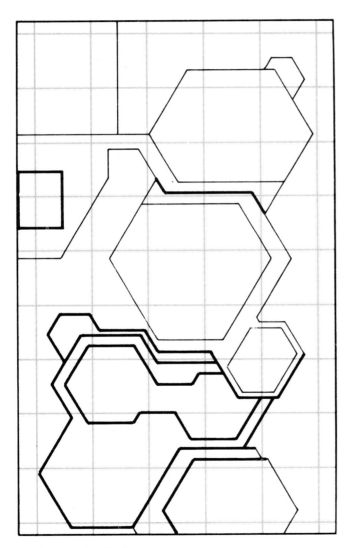

Setting-out plan. Each square represents 2 × 2 m.

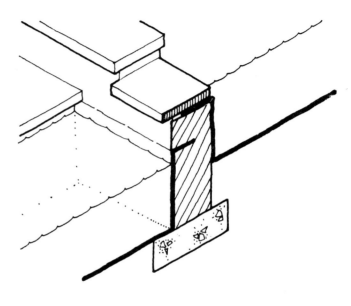

Waterfall: Build pools on two levels, lining them with either butyl or waterproof render.

It is important to provide sufficient lip or overhang, say 5 cm (2 in.), in order to throw the water into the lower pool. The wider the waterfall, the more powerful must be the pump (submersible) to recirculate the water and to throw it over the fall.

22 Garden with a Swimming Pool

Can a swimming pool be accommodated in a garden of modest size without spoiling its appearance? No problem – if it is tackled in a sensible way. In the garden we have designed, the whole of the swimming pool area has been accommodated in the rear half of the plot, leaving the front half intact as a garden. But this does not prevent the pool being sited in pleasant surroundings.

Assuming that the average depth of the pool is two metres (6 feet) – it will probably be one metre (three feet) at the shallow end and two and a half or three metres (eight or nine feet) at the deep end – it follows that if the pool is excavated to an average depth of one metre (four feet), that volume of soil is available to be spread around the site to raise the surrounding level by 60 cm (2 ft), leaving the pool at the desired depth. It is therefore approached from the garden area by four 15-cm (6-in..) steps.

A swimming pool needs filtering and probably (in a temperate climate) heating as well, so provision is made for a shed to house the equipment. A changing room is also desirable and this is placed in the far corner. Between these two sheds a series of solar heating panels has been sited. These are at their most efficient in summer, and can greatly reduce heating costs. On two sides the pool is sheltered by a variety of flowering shrubs – an extension, in fact, of the border bounding the path and lawn of the garden below.

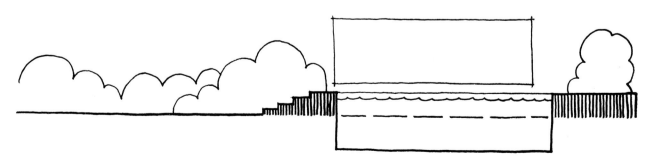

This section sketch indicates why it is unneccessary to expend time, labour and perhaps money in excavating to the full depth of the intended pool. A large amount – up to half – of the removed soil can be used to build up the surrounding ground to give the full depth required. This technique also solves the problem of disposing of the excavated soil.

1 Changing Room/Summerhouse

2 Plant/filter room

3 Solar Heating panels

4 Refuse

5 Steps

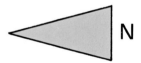 Lawn

Pool

Paving

Shrubs over 1.8 m (6 ft)

Shrubs 1–2 m (3–6 ft)

Ground cover or
Herbaceous plants

N

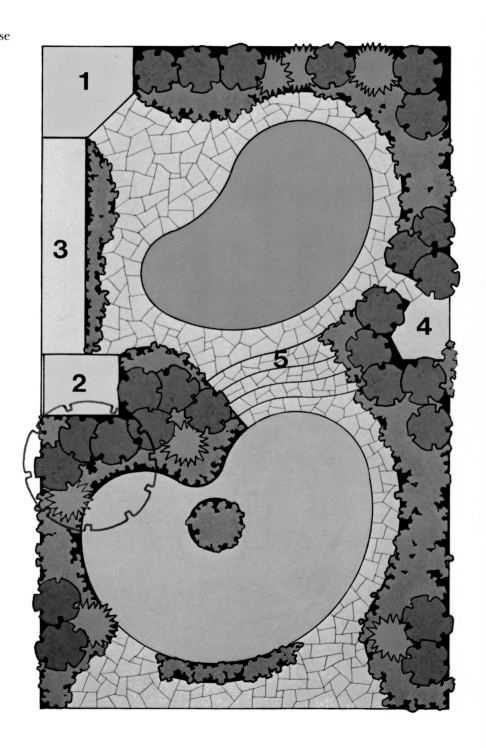

*The curving shape of the pool is echoed
by that of the lawn, which affords a
pleasant, well-sheltered place for
sunbathing after the swim.*

On the opposing side another border culminates
in thickly planted shrubs, dominated by an
ornamental tree to conceal the utility part of the
pool area.

The siting of the pool in the back half of the
garden, its elevated position, and its partial
concealment by planting on each side of the steps
all combine to mould it unobtrusively into the
garden scene.

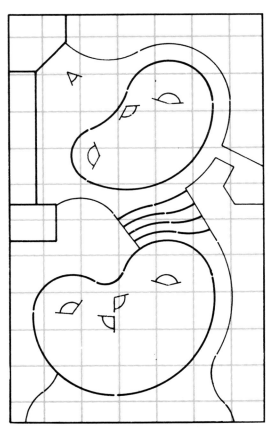

Setting-out plan showing radial points. Each square represents 2 × 2 m.

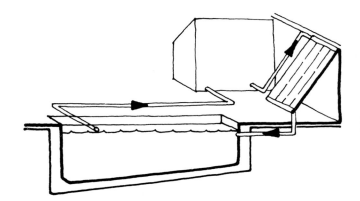

Diagram right shows only the principle of the mechanical plant required. The construction of the pool and the installation of the plant should be left to a reputable swimming pool contractor.

To ensure a high standard of hygiene, the water in the pool must be regularly filtered and this is done by pumping the water out of the pool and through a filter housed in a suitable shed, and returning it to the pool via underground pipes.

A gas or oil boiler can also be installed and connected to the system to heat the pool water, but solar panels have been proved to be most effective in warming pool water in the summer months, and save the cost of gas or oil fuel.

The panels must face within 5 degrees of due south for maximum efficiency. Their area should be about half the surface area of the pool, but take advice from the manufacturers. The series of panels can easily be connected to the filter system and require no pump or pipework of their own.

It is essential to cover the pool at night with an insulating floating blanket in all but the warmest weather to keep the heat in. Room should be made in the shed for chemicals, nets and vacuuming equipment for cleaning the pool walls and floor.

GARDEN PLANT CHOICE

ORNAMENTAL TREES

Plant name	Species or variety	Deciduous/ evergreen	Ultimate height	Flowering period	Characteristics
Acer	griseum (paperbark maple)	Deciduous	5 m + (16 ft +)	—	Orange-brown, peeling bark, attractive in winter
	negundo 'variegatum' (ash-leafed maple)	Deciduous	8 m + (26 ft +)	—	Leaves conspicuously bordered silvery-white
	pseudoplatanus 'Brilliantissimum'	Deciduous	5 m + (16 ft +)	—	Young foliage glowing shrimp-pink in spring
Arbutus	unedo (strawberry tree)	Evergreen	5 m (16 ft)	Sept.–Nov.	Small, bell-shaped white flowers; red fruit
Betula	pendula (silver birch)	Deciduous	20 m (66 ft)	—	A graceful tree with white bark; autumn tints
	p. Youngii	Deciduous	6 m (20 ft)	—	This is a more weeping form of silver birch
Catalpa	bignonioides (Indian bean tree)	Deciduous	6 m + (20 ft +)	July–Aug.	Large, heart-shaped leaves; white flowers
Cercis	siliquastrum (Judas tree)	Deciduous	8 m + (26 ft +)	April–May	Rosy-lilac flowers are produced on bare branches
Cotoneaster	hybridus pendulus	Semi-evergreen	5 m + (16 ft +)	May–June	Cascades of red berries in autumn and winter
Crataegus	oxyacantha (syn. coccinea plena) 'Paul's Scarlet'	Deciduous	5 m (16 ft)	May	A double, scarlet form of the May or Hawthorn
Gleditsia	triacanthos 'Sunburst'	Deciduous	6 m (20 ft)	—	A striking tree with bright yellow young foliage
Ilex (holly)	aquifolium	Evergreen	10 m + (33 ft +)	—	The common holly; berries only on female trees
	a. 'Golden King'	Evergreen	4 m + (13 ft +)	—	Bold yellow margins; produces attractive berries

ORNAMENTAL TREES (continued)

Plant name	Species or variety	Deciduous/ evergreen	Ultimate height	Flowering period	Characteristics
	a. 'J. C. van Tol'	Evergreen	4 m + (13 ft +)	—	An almost spineless form; good for berries
	a. pyramidalis	Evergreen	4 m + (13 ft +)	—	Pyramidal in outline, and free-fruiting
Laburnum	alpinum (Scotch laburnum)	Deciduous	8 m + (26 ft +)	May–June	Lovely yellow tassels of bright yellow flowers
	'Vossii'	Deciduous	6 m + (20 ft +)	May–June	This is a beautiful form and very free-flowering
Liquidambar	styraciflua (sweet gum)	Deciduous	6 m + (20 ft +)	—	Grown for its spectacular crimson autumn colour
Magnolia	soulangiana	Deciduous	6 m (20 ft)	April	Huge white flowers, stained petunia at base
	stellata	Deciduous	4 m (13 ft)	March–April	Star-like white flowers, very freely produced
Malus (crab apple)	floribunda	Deciduous	6 m (20 ft)	April	Red in bud opening to pink-flushed white blossom
	'Golden Hornet'	Deciduous	6 m (20 ft)	April–May	Clusters of small yellow fruit that lasts well
	'John Downie'	Deciduous	10 m (33 ft)	April–May	Very attractive orange and red edible fruit
	'Profusion'	Deciduous	6 m (20 ft)	April–May	Red blossom freely produced; young leaves purple
	sargentii	Deciduous	3 m (10 ft)	April	White blossom followed by small red fruit
Parrotia	persica	Deciduous	5 m (16 ft)	Jan.–March	Grown mainly for its rich autumn colour
Prunus	dulcis (common almond)	Deciduous	8 m (26 ft)	March	Early and very reliable; clear pink flowers
	cerasifera 'Pissardii'	Deciduous	7 m (23 ft)	April	Plum-coloured foliage; pinkish-white blossom
	persica 'Prince Charming' (peach)	Deciduous	5 m (16 ft)	April	Double, rose-red flowers borne on naked stems

ORNAMENTAL TREES (continued)

Plant name	Species or variety	Deciduous/ evergreen	Ultimate height	Flowering period	Characteristics
	'Pink Perfection' (cherry)	Deciduous	6 m (20 ft)	April–May	Bright pink buds open to paler, double blossom
	'Shirotae' (cherry)	Deciduous	6 m (20 ft)	April–May	Large, semi-double, snow-white, fragrant flowers
	subhirtella autumnalis	Deciduous	6 m (20 ft)	Nov.–March	Pale pink, semi-double blossom on bare stems
Pyrus	salicifolia pendula (willow-leafed pear)	Deciduous	5 m (16 ft)	April	Silver-grey, willow-like leaves; white flowers
Rhus	typhina (stag's horn sumach)	Deciduous	5 m (16 ft)	—	Large, divided leaves turn orange-red in autumn
Robinia	pseudoacacia 'Frisia'	Deciduous	6 m (20 ft)	—	Bright yellow, pinnate leaves spring to autumn
Salix	purpurea pendula	Deciduous	5 m (16 ft)	—	Small weeping tree with long, pendulous branches
Sorbus	aria lutescens (whitebeam)	Deciduous	10 m (33 ft)	—	Leaves open with a white felt, later grey-green
	aucuparia (mountain ash)	Deciduous	12 m (39 ft)	May–June	Creamy-white flowers and orange-red berries

CONIFERS

Plant name	Species or variety	Deciduous/ evergreen	Ultimate height	Hedging	Characteristics
Cedrus	atlantica glauca (blue cedar)	Evergreen	30 m + (98 ft +)	No	A magnificent conifer with grey-blue foliage
	deodara aurea (golden Deodar)	Evergreen	20 m (66 ft)	No	Golden-yellow in spring, becoming greenish
Chamaecyparis	lawsoniana (Lawson's cypress)	Evergreen	30 m + (98 ft +)	Yes	Dark green, fan-like sprays of foliage; good screen
	l. columnaris	Evergreen	9 m (30 ft)	No	A narrow form with attractive blue-grey foliage

ORNAMENTAL TREES (continued)

Plant name	Species or variety	Deciduous/evergreen	Ultimate height	Flowering period	Characteristics
	l. 'Fletcheri'	Evergreen	7 m (23 ft)	Yes	Grey-green, feathery foliage
	l. 'Green Hedger'	Evergreen	20 m (66 ft)	Yes	Makes a dense hedge of rich green foliage
	l. lanei	Evergreen	15 m (49 ft)	Yes	Feathery sprays of rich gold; cone-shaped
	l. lutea	Evergreen	12 m (39 ft)	Yes	Large, flattened sprays of yellow foliage
Cryptomeria	japonica 'Elegans'	Evergreen	8 m (26 ft)	No	Feathery; deep rose tints in autumn and winter
x Cupressocyparis	leylandii (Leyland cypress)	Evergreen	30 m (98 ft)	Yes	The fastest-growing conifer; makes a tall hedge
Ginkgo	biloba (maidenhair tree)	Deciduous	20 m + (66 ft +)	No	Distinctive, five-lobed leaves; yellow in autumn
Juniperus	chinensis aurea (Chinese juniper)	Evergreen	8 m (26 ft)	No	Dainty yellow foliage; forms a slender column
	communis hibernica (Irish juniper)	Evergreen	5 m (16 ft)	No	Forms a slender but dense column; rich green
	c. repanda	Evergreen	1.5 m (5 ft)	No	This is a very useful ground-hugging juniper
Picea	abies (Christmas tree)	Evergreen	30 m + (98 ft +)	No	The popular Christmas tree needs no description
	breweriana (Brewer's weeping spruce)	Evergreen	20 m (66 ft)	No	Forms a green fountain of long, drooping branches
	pungens 'Koster'	Evergreen	10 m (33 ft)	No	A conical tree with silver-blue foliage
Taxus	baccata (yew)	Evergreen	15 m + (49 ft +)	Yes	Dark green foliage; makes a superb hedge
Thuja	occidentalis 'Holmstrupii'	Evergreen	4 m (13 ft)	No	A narrowly conical, slow-growing tree; rich green
	o. lutescens	Evergreen	5 m (16 ft)	No	Pale, yellowish-green flattened sprays; conical

SHRUBS

There is a vast range of shrubs from which to choose, and selection must inevitably be based partly on personal taste and partly on the special requirements of the plants (especially soil). The following list embraces what we consider to be the more desirable shrubs for the gardens in this book. You will find those requiring a lime-free soil, and those that can be regarded as 'below-eye-level' (low-growing) shrubs, listed in separate tables.

Plant name	Species or variety	Deciduous/ evergreen	Ultimate height	Flowering period	Characteristics
Aralia	elata (Japanese angelica tree)	Deciduous	4 m (13 ft)	Aug.–Sept.	Huge, pinnate leaves; sprays of white flowers
Arundinaria	japonica (bamboo)	Evergreen	4 m (13 ft)	—	Willow-like foliage on bamboo canes; dense growth
Berberis	darwinii	Evergreen	2 m (6½ ft)	April–May	Masses of small golden flowers; blue berries
	stenophylla	Evergreen	3 m (10 ft)	April–May	Arching branches studded with yellow flowers
Buddleia	alternifolia	Deciduous	4 m (13 ft)	June–July	Produces a cascade of arching branches; mauve
	davidii 'Royal Red'	Deciduous	4 m (13 ft)	July–Aug.	Red-purple spikes of flowers on arching stems
Choisya	ternata (Mexican orange blossom)	Evergreen	3 m (10 ft)	May	Fragrant white flowers set against glossy leaves
Cornus	mas (Cornelian cherry)	Deciduous	5 m (16 ft)	Feb.	Masses of small yellow flowers on bare stems
Cortaderia	selloana (syn. argentea) (pampas grass)	Evergreen	3 m (10 ft)	Sept.–Nov.	Tall, silvery plumes above large spiky leaves
Corylus	avellana contorta (corkscrew hazel)	Deciduous	5 m (16 ft)	Feb.–March	Quaintly twisted branches and yellow catkins

SHRUBS (continued)

Plant name	Species or variety	Deciduous/evergreen	Ultimate height	Flowering period	Characteristics
Cotoneaster	franchetii sternianus	Semi-evergreen	4 m (13 ft)	May–June	Small pink flowers followed by orange-red berries
Cytisus	battandieri	Deciduous	5 m (16 ft)	June	Cone-shaped clusters of fragrant, yellow flowers
Elaeagnus	pungens maculata	Evergreen	4 m (13 ft)	—	Leaves are boldly splashed with bright yellow
Escallonia	'Donard Brilliance'	Evergreen	2 m (6½ ft)	June–July	Arching branches of crimson flowers; glossy leaves
Fatsia	japonica	Evergreen	3 m (10 ft)	Oct.–Nov.	Bold, hand-shaped leaves; milky-white flowers
Forsythia	'Lynwood' (golden bell bush)	Deciduous	3 m (10 ft)	March–April	A mass of rich yellow flowers on erect branches
Hamamelis	mollis (Chinese witch hazel)	Deciduous	5 m (16 ft)	Dec.–March	Sweetly fragrant, yellow flowers on naked branches
Hibiscus	syriacus 'Blue Bird' (tree hollyhock)	Deciduous	2 m (6½ ft)	Aug.–Sept.	Large violet-blue flowers with dark eyes; striking
	s. 'Woodbridge'	Deciduous	2 m (6½ ft)	Aug.–Sept.	A variety with handsome rose-pink flowers
Hypericum	'Hidcote'	Semi-evergreen	2 m (6½ ft)	July.–Aug.	Large, golden yellow, saucer-shaped flowers
Kolkwitzia	amabilis 'Pink Cloud' (beauty bush)	Deciduous	2 m (6½ ft)	May–June	Bell-like, soft pink flowers on feathery branches
Lonicera	nitida 'Baggesen's Gold' (Chinese honeysuckle)	Evergreen	4 m (13 ft)	—	Small, golden leaves becoming greenish in autumn
Mahonia	'Charity'	Evergreen	3 m (10 ft)	Jan.–Feb.	Terminal clusters of fragrant, yellow flowers
	japonica	Evergreen	2 m (6½ ft)	Feb.–March	Fragrant, yellow flowers; attractive leaves
Osmanthus	delavayi	Evergreen	3 m (10 ft)	April	Small, white flowers; fragrant; spreading habit

SHRUBS (continued)

Plant name	Species or variety	Deciduous/ evergreen	Ultimate height	Flowering period	Characteristics
Philadelphus (mock orange)	'Enchantment'	Deciduous	4 m (13 ft)	June–July	Arching ropes of fragrant white flowers
Phormium	tenax (New Zealand flax)	Evergreen	3 m (10 ft)	—	Sword-shaped leaves, producing a striking effect
Ribes	sanguineum 'Pulborough Scarlet' (flowering currant)	Deciduous	3 m (10 ft)	March–April	Racemes of rich red flowers; a fast grower
Sambucus	nigra aurea (golden elder)	Deciduous	5 m (16 ft)	—	Golden yellow leaves, tending to deepen with age
Spartium	junceum (Spanish broom)	Deciduous	3 m (10 ft)	June–Aug.	Yellow flowers shaped like those of the pea
Spiraea	x arguta (bridal wreath)	Deciduous	3 m (10 ft)	April	Tall, arching sprays of small, white flowers
	x bumalda 'Anthony Waterer'	Deciduous	2 m (6½ ft)	July–Sept.	Broad, flattened heads of tiny carmine flowers
	x b. 'Goldflame'	Deciduous	2 m (6½ ft)	July–Aug.	Young growth gold, turning more green later
Symphoricarpos	albus (snowberry)	Deciduous	3 m (10 ft)	July	Small rosy flowers are followed by white berries
Syringa	vulgaris 'Madame Lemoine' (lilac)	Deciduous	6 m (20 ft)	May	Creamy-white buds open to pure white; double
	v. 'Michael Buchner'	Deciduous	6 m (20 ft)	May	A double lilac with pale, rose-lilac flowers
	v. 'Mrs Edward Harding'	Deciduous	6 m (20 ft)	May	A semi-double variety with claret-red flowers
	v. 'Souvenir de Louis Spaeth'	Deciduous	6 m (20 ft)	May	Single, wine-red blooms; a reliable variety
Tamarix	pentandra (tamarisk)	Deciduous	5 m (16 ft)	Aug.	The bush becomes a foaming mass of pink flowers
Viburnum	fragrans	Deciduous	4 m (13 ft)	Nov.–Feb.	Fragrant, white flowers tinged with pink

SHRUBS (continued)

Plant name	Species or variety	Deciduous/evergreen	Ultimate height	Flowering period	Characteristics
	x juddii	Deciduous	2 m (6½ ft)	April–May	Clusters of sweetly scented pale pink flowers
	opulus sterile (snowball bush)	Deciduous	5 m (16 ft)	May–June	White flowers held in ball-shaped heads
	tinus (laurustinus)	Evergreen	4 m (13 ft)	Dec.–April	White flowers, pink in bud; blooms winter

LOW-GROWING SHRUBS (below-eye-level shrubs)

Plant name	Species or variety	Deciduous/evergeen	Ultimate height	Flowering period	Characteristics
Berberis	thunbergii atropurpurea	Deciduous	1.5 m (5 ft)	May	Reddish-purple foliage, colours more in autumn
Cornus	alba sibirica (Westonbirt dogwood)	Deciduous	1.5 m (5 ft)	June	Sealing-wax red stems in winter; autumn colour
Cotoneaster	horizontalis	Deciduous	1.8 m (6 ft)	June	Wall or ground cover; abundant red berries
Cytisus	x praecox	Deciduous	1.8 m (6 ft)	April–May	A spectacular, tumbling mass of cream
Daphne	mezereum	Deciduous	1.5 m (5 ft)	Feb –March	Small mauve flowers; an exquisite fragrance
Fuchsia	'Madame Cornelissen'	Deciduous	1.8 m (6 ft)	July–Oct.	Large-flowered, red and white; may need shelter
	'Mrs Popple'	Deciduous	1.5 m (5 ft)	July–Oct.	A hardy variety; scarlet sepals, violet petals
Hydrangea	macrophylla Hortensia type	Deciduous	1.8 m (6 ft)	July–Sept.	These are the well-known 'mophead' hydrangeas
	Lacecap type	Deciduous	1.8 m (6 ft)	July–Sept.	The coloured ray florets form a ring round edge
Hypericum	calycinum	Evergreen	30 cm (1 ft)	July–Aug.	Large golden flowers; a fine ground cover

LOW-GROWING SHRUBS (below-eye-level shrubs) (continued)

Plant name	Species or variety	Deciduous/ evergreen	Ultimate height	Flowering period	Characteristics
Lavandula (lavender)	'Munstead'	Evergreen	75 cm (2½ ft)	July	Compact plant; lavender-blue flowers; aromatic
	'Twickel Purple'	Evergreen	75 cm (2½ ft)	July	Grey-green aromatic lavender-blue flowers
Mahonia	aquifolium	Evergreen	1.8 m (6 ft)	March–April	Clusters of yellow flowers; decorative leaves
Philadelphus	'Manteau d'Hermine'	Deciduous	1.5 m (5 ft)	June	Dainty, double, white flowers; good fragrance
Potentilla	'Elizabeth'	Deciduous	1.5 m (5 ft)	June–Oct.	Forms a dome-shaped bush; primrose yellow flowers
	'Katherine Dykes'	Deciduous	1.5 m (5 ft)	June–Oct.	Covered with canary yellow flowers all summer
	'Red Ace'	Deciduous	75 cm (2½ ft)	June–Oct.	Vermilion petals, under surface pale yellow
Prunus	laurocerasus 'Otto Luyken'	Evergreen	1.5 m (5 ft)	April	White, candle-like flower spikes; shiny leaves
Santolina	chamaecyparissus nana (cotton lavender)	Evergreen	75 cm (2½ ft)	June–July	Silver-grey, woolly foliage; yellow flowers
Senecio	laxifolius	Evergreen	90 cm (3 ft)	June–July	Silver-grey, woolly leaves; yellow daisy flowers
Weigela	florida variegata	Deciduous	1.5 m (5 ft)	June	Cream-edged leaves; clear, pale pink flowers
	'Bristol Ruby'	Deciduous	1.8 m (6 ft)	June	A very free-flowering variety with red flowers
Yucca	filamentosa	Evergreen	1.8 m (6 ft)	July–Aug.	Sword-like leaves; impressive creamy flower spike
	flaccida 'Ivory'	Evergreen	1.8 m (6 ft)	July–Aug.	Spiky leaves with curly white threads; striking

SHRUBS FOR A LIME-FREE SOIL

These shrubs can still be grown where lime exists, in beds of acid, lime-free soil built up at least 30 cm (1 ft) above ground level. Alternatively they can be planted in containers filled with a similar mixture. If the lime content of the soil is only slightly excessive, the plants can be treated annually with sequestered iron.

Low-growing shrubs (below eye level) are indicated by an asterisk*

Plant name	Species or variety	Deciduous/ evergreen	Ultimate height	Flowering period	Characteristics
*Azalea	luteum	Deciduous	1.5 m (f ft)	May–June	Orange-yellow, funnel-shaped flowers; fragrant
*	Knaphill, Exbury hybrids	Deciduous	1.8 m (6 ft)	May	Wide colour range and good autumn colour
*	Kurume and other hybrids	Evergreen	90 cm (3 ft)	April–May	Most form a mass of small flowers; need shade
*	mollis hybrids	Deciduous	1.5 m (5 ft)	May	Trusses of large flowers in various colours
Camellia	japonica 'Adolphe Audusson'	Evergreen	3 m (10 ft)	March–April	Semi-double, blood red with conspicuous stamens
	j. 'Lady Vansittart'	Evergreen	3 m (10 ft)	March–April	Semi-double flowers, white striped with pink
	x williamsii 'Donation'	Evergreen	3 m (10 ft)	April	Large, semi-double deep pink flowers; erect
	x w. 'Francis Hanger'	Evergreen	3 m (10 ft)	March–April	A striking single white; erect growth habit
	x w. 'J. C. Williams'	Evergreen	3 m (10 ft)	March–April	A beautiful camellia; large, single pink blooms
*Kalmia	latifolia (calico bush)	Evergreen	1.8 m (6 ft)	June	Rose-coloured flowers set against glossy leaves
*Pernettya	mucronata	Evergreen	90 cm (3 ft)	April	Pink, red or white berries on female; needs male
Pieris	'Forest Flame'	Evergreen	2 m (6½ ft)	April	Brilliant red young leaves; creamy flowers
	formosa forrestii 'Wakehurst'	Evergreen	3 m (10 ft)	April	Young foliage resembles bright red flowers
*Rhododendron (species)	impeditum	Evergreen	45 cm (1½ ft)	April	Blue flowers carried over small, oval leaves

SHRUBS FOR LIME-FREE SOIL (continued)

Plant name	Species or variety	Deciduous/ evergreen	Ultimate height	Flowering period	Characteristics
*	praecox	Evergreen	1.5 m (5 ft)	Feb.–March	Actually a hybrid; translucent rosy-purple
*	williamsianum	Evergreen	45 cm (1½ ft)	April–May	Coin-shaped leaves; pink, bell-shaped flowers
*	yakushimanum	Evergreen	1.2 m (4 ft)	May	Pink buds, opening to white; leathery leaves
Rhododendron (large-flowered hybrids)	'Betty Wormald'	Evergreen	1.5 m + (5 ft +)	April–June	Immense trusses of large, pink, frilled flowers
	'Britannia'	Evergreen	1.5 m + (5 ft +)	April–June	Gloxinia-shaped glowing crimson trusses
	'Cynthia'	Evergreen	1.5m + (5 ft +)	April–June	Widely funnel-shaped deep rose flowers
	'Kluis Sensation'	Evergreen	1.5 m + (5 ft +)	April–June	Bright scarlet flowers with darker spots
	'Mrs John Millais'	Evergreen	1.5 m + (5 ft +)	April–June	Pink buds open to reveal lovely white blooms
	'Purple Splendour'	Evergreen	1.5 m + (5 ft +)	April–June	Funnel-shaped, purple-blue with black markings
*Rhododendron (dwarf hybrids)	'Blue Tit'	Evergreen	90 cm (3 ft)	April–May	Soft blue, open bells, intensifying with age
*	'Carmen'	Evergreen	45 cm (1½ ft)	May	Waxy, blood red, bell-shaped flowers; low growing
*	'Elizabeth'	Evergreen	1.5 m (5 ft)	April–May	Orange-red, trumpet-shaped flowers

SHRUB ROSES

Species or variety	Ultimate height	Colour	Characteristics
Rosa x alba (white rose of York)	3 m (10 ft)	White	Richly scented, semi-double, about 7.5 cm (3 in)
R. 'Canary Bird'	2 m (6½ ft)	Butter yellow	Saucer-shaped blooms on arching stems, in May
R. centifolia (cabbage rose)	2 m (6½ ft)	Pink	Large, double, richly scented; fragrant leaves
R. gallica officinalis (red rose of Lancaster)	1.5 m (5 ft)	Crimson	Semi-double, richly fragrant; prominent anthers
Hybrid musk 'Cornelia'	3 m (10 ft)	Rose pink	Makes a wide, sturdy bush with good foliage
'Elmshorn'	3 m (10 ft)	Crimson	Large trusses of cup-shaped blooms; brilliant
'Penelope'	3 m (10 ft)	Shell pink	Clusters of semi-double blooms; red hips
R. 'Nevada'	3 m (10 ft)	Creamy white	Arching stems with large, single flowers
R. rugosa 'Frau Dagmar Hastrop'	1.8 m (6 ft)	Pale pink	Heavy crop of crimson hips; makes a good hedge
'Roseraie de l'Hay'	1.8 m (6 ft)	Reddish purple	Double flowers about 10 cm (4 in) across
'Sarah van Fleet'	2 m (6½ ft)	Soft pink	Flowers continuously from June to Sept.

CLIMBERS AND WALL SHRUBS

Plant name	Species or variety	Deciduous/ evergreen	Ultimate height	Best aspect	Flowering period	Characteristics
Campsis (trumpet vine)	grandiflora	Deciduous	6 m (20 ft)	S–W	Aug.–Sept.	Trumpet-shaped, orange-red flowers; unusual
	radicans	Deciduous	6 m (20 ft)	S–W	Aug.–Sept.	Clusters of orange and scarlet flowers
Ceanothus (Californian lilac)	'Burkwoodii'	Evergreen	3 m (10 ft)	S–W	July–Sept.	Rich, dark blue flowers on a rounded bush
	'Delight'	Evergreen	3 m (10 ft)	S–W	May	Long, strong blue panicles; a hardy variety

CLIMBERS AND WALL SHRUBS (continued)

Plant name	Species or variety	Deciduous/ evergreen	Ultimate height	Best aspect	Flowering period	Characteristics
Chaenomeles (flowering quince)	x superba 'Crimson and Gold'	Deciduous	2 m (6½ ft)	Any	March–April	Deep crimson with contrasting golden anthers
	x s. 'Knap Hill Scarlet'	Deciduous	2 m (6½ ft)	Any	March–April	Profusion of bright orange-scarlet flowers
Clematis	flammula (Virgin's Bower)	Deciduous	8 m + (26 ft +)	Any	Aug.–Oct.	White, sweetly-scented flowers; silky seed heads
	x jackmanii	Deciduous	5 m + (16 ft +)	E–S–W	July–Oct.	Large, violet-purple flowers borne in profusion
	montana	Deciduous	8 m + (26 ft +)	Any	April–May	Profusion of white flowers 5 cm (2 in) across
	m. rubens	Deciduous	8 m + (26 ft +)	Any	April–May	A pink form with bronze-purple young shoots
	patens	Deciduous	5 m + (16 ft +)	E–S–W	May–June	Creamy-white flowers, 10–15 cm (4–6 in) across
	viticella	Deciduous	5 m + (16 ft +)	E–S–W	July–Oct.	Violet, blue, or reddish-purple flowers
Garrya	elliptica	Evergreen	3 m (10 ft)	N–E	Jan.–Feb.	Silky, grey-green catkins, best on male plants
Hedera (ivy)	canariensis	Evergreen	8 m + (26 ft +)	Any	—	Large, bright, glossy leaves, strong-growing
	colchica dentata variegata	Evergreen	8 m + (26 ft +)	Any	—	Large leaves shaded green, cream, grey, yellow
	helix 'Buttercup'	Evergreen	8 m + (26 ft +)	Any	—	New leaves golden yellow, greener with age

CLIMBERS AND WALL SHRUBS (continued)

Plant name	Species or variety	Deciduous/ evergreen	Ultimate height	Best aspect	Flowering period	Characteristics
Hydrangea	petiolaris	Deciduous	8 m + (26 ft +)	N–E–W	June–July	Heads of white flowers like lacecap hydrangeas
Jasminum	nudiflorum (winter jasmine)	Deciduous	4 m (13 ft)	Any	Nov.–March	Butter-yellow flowers set against green stems
	officinale (sweet jasmine)	Dediduous	8 m (26 ft)	Any	June–Aug.	Twining climber with fragrant white flowers
Lonicera (honeysuckle)	x americana	Deciduous	3 m + (10 ft +)	E–S–W	June–Sept.	Profusion of rose-apricot, fragrant flowers
	japonica 'Halliana'	Evergreen	6 m + (20 ft +)	E–S–W	June–Oct.	Creamy biscuit coloured, and very fragrant
	periclymenum 'Serotina' (late Dutch honeysuckle)	Deciduous	3 m + 10 ft +)	E–S–W	July–Sept.	Reddish purple and yellow; heavy fragrance
Parthenocissus	henryana	Deciduous	9 m (30 ft)	N–W	—	Dark green leaves with silvery variagation
	quinquefolia (Virginia creeper)	Deciduous	9 m (30 ft)	Any	—	Brilliant scarlet autumn colour, self-clinging
Polygonum	baldschuanicum (Russian vine)	Deciduous	7.5 m + (25 ft +)	Any	July–Oct.	Foaming mass of small white flowers; vigorous
Rosa	various climbers and ramblers	Deciduous	3 m + (10 ft +)	S–W	May–Oct.	'Perpetual flowering' type are best; use ramblers for pillars and pergolas
Vitis (vine)	coignetiae	Deciduous	9 m + (30 ft +)	S–W	June–July	Really huge leaves, with rich autumn colours
	vinifera 'Brandt'	Deciduous	9 m + (30 ft +)	S–W	June–July	Purple grapes; good leaf colour; edible

CLIMBERS AND WALL SHRUBS (continued)

Plant name	Species or variety	Deciduous/ evergreen	Ultimate height	Best aspect	Flowering period	Characteristics
Wisteria	sinensis	Deciduous	9 m + (30 ft +)	S–W	May–June	Long racemes of fragrant, pale lilac flowers

GROUND COVER

Plant name	Species or variety	Height	Flowering period	Characteristics
Ajuga (bugle)	reptans atropurpurea	10 cm (4 in)	May–June	Forms a reddish-purple carpet; blue flowers
	r. variegata	15 cm (6 in)	May–June	White and grey variegation; blue flowers
Alchemilla	mollis (lady's mantle)	45 cm (1½ ft)	June–July	Soft sprays of yellow-green flowers; round leaves
Artemisia (wormwood)	'Lambrook Silver'	90 cm (3 ft)	—	A robust plant with silvery-grey foliage
	'Silver Queen'	60 cm (2 ft)	—	Attractive, silvery, divided leaves; bushy
Aubrieta	various varieties; colours include blues, purples, reds, and pinks	15 cm (6 in)	April–May	Forms a dense cushion; cut back after flowering
Bergenia (elephant ears)	'Ballawley'	30 cm (1 ft)	April–May	Large, thick leaves; red stems; rose-red flowers
	cordifolia	30 cm (1 ft)	March–April	Large, heart-shaped leaves; deep pink flowers
Brunnera	macrophylla (perennial forget-me-not)	45 cm (1½ ft)	April–June	Heart-shaped leaves and sprays of blue flowers
Campanula	portenschlagiana	10 cm (4 in)	June–Sept.	Masses of deep blue flowers on trailing stems
Dianthus (pink)	allwoodii 'Ian'	30 cm (1 ft)	June–Aug.	Glowing crimson flowers against greyish leaves
	deltoides	10 cm (4 in)	June–Aug.	Brilliant scarlet blooms over green foliage

GROUND COVER (continued)

Plant name	Species or variety	Height	Flowering period	Characteristics
	'Doris'	30 cm (1 ft)	June–Sept.	Succession of warm pink flowers with deeper centre
Geranium	endressii 'Wargrave Pink'	45 cm (1½ ft)	May–Sept.	Clear, silvery-pink flowers in profusion
	'Johnson's Blue'	45 cm (1½ ft)	May–Sept.	Masses of cup-shaped, bright blue flowers
	sanguineum lancastrense 'Splendens'	25 cm (10 in)	June–Sept.	Rose-pink flowers on plant of spreading habit
Helianthemum (rock rose)	Many varieties; mostly pinks or yellows	10–15 cm (4–6 in)	June–Aug.	Evergreen, usually greyish, foliage; best in sun
Helleborus	niger (Christmas rose)	30 cm (1 ft)	Jan.–Feb.	White, open flowers with golden stamens
	orientalis (Lenten rose)	45 cm (1½ ft)	Feb.–April	White, plum, or maroon flowers; fingered foliage
Hosta (Plantain lily)	fortunei	60 cm (2 ft)	July–Aug.	Large, handsome leaves; lilac flower spikes
	f. albo marginata	75 cm (2½ ft)	July–Aug.	Leaves prettily edged with cream variegation
	f. aurea marginata	75 cm (2½ ft)	July–Aug.	Leaves edged light yellow; mauve flower spikes
	sieboldiana	60 cm (2 ft)	July–Aug.	Large, blue-green leaves; lilac-mauve flowers
Hypericum	calycinum (see low-growing-shrubs list)			
	coris	15 cm (6 in)	June–Sept.	Golden yellow flowers 12 mm (½ in) across
Iberis	sempervirens (perennial candytuft)	15 cm (6 in)	May	Compact evergreen mounds; pure white flowers
Lamium	galeobdolon variegatum (dead nettle)	25 cm (10 in)	April–June	White-variegated leaves and yellow flowers
	maculatum 'Beacon Silver'	10 cm (4 in)	April–June	Outstanding silver-white foliage; pink flowers
Lavandula (lavender)	(see low-growing-shrubs list)			

GROUND COVER (continued)

Plant name	Species or variety	Height	Flowering period	Characteristics
Pachysandra	terminalis	15 cm (6 in)	May	Dwarf evergreen with white flowers; not invasive
Polygonum (knotgrass)	affine 'Donald Lowndes'	25 cm (10 in)	Aug.–Oct.	Small red spikes, coppery foliage in autumn
	vaccinifolium	10 cm (4 in)	Aug.–Oct.	Pink spikes over bronzy-green leaves; creeping
Santolina	(see low-growing-shrubs list)			
Saxifraga	umbrosa (London pride)	20 cm (8 in)	April–May	Pink flowers rising from evergreen rosettes
Sedum (stonecrop)	'Coral Carpet'	10 cm (4 in)	July–Aug.	Grey foliage forming hummocks; yellow flowers
	maximum atropurpureum	45 cm (1½ ft)	Aug.–Sept.	Striking red leaves; head of pink flowers
	'Ruby Glow'	20 cm (8 in)	July–Sept.	Ruby-coloured flowers over purple-grey foliage
	spectabile (ice plant)	45 cm (1½ ft)	Aug.–Oct.	Plates of pink flowers over pale, fleshy leaves
Stachys	byzantinus	45 cm (1½ ft)	July–Aug.	Deep pink flowers over silvery, woolly foliage
	lanata (lambs' ears)	45 cm (1½ ft)	July–Aug.	Woolly, silver foliage; pink flower spikes
Thymus (thyme)	serpyllum albus	2.5 cm (1 in)	June–Aug.	Snow-white flowers over pale green foliage
	s. 'Annie Hall'	5 cm (2 in)	June–July	Dainty, very pale pink flowers on green mat
	s. coccineus	5 cm (2 in)	June–Aug.	Bright, rose red flowers; dark green leaves
Tiarella	cordifolia (foam flower)	20 cm (8 in)	May–July	Creamy-white spikes over heart-shaped leaves
Vinca (periwinkle)	major	25 cm (10 in)	April–May	Trailing evergreen with blue flowers; rampant
	minor	15 cm (6 in)	April–May	A smaller-leaved version; bright blue flowers
	m. aureo variegata	15 cm (6 in)	April–May	Gold-variegated foliage; white flowers